UNDEFEATED AGENTS

WARFARE STRATEGIES FOR THE INTERCESSOR AND SUPERNATURAL INTERCESSION

SARAH FLOWERS

Undefeated Agents
Warfare Strategies for the Intercessor and
Supernatural intercession
Sarah Flowers

© 2021, Sarah Flowers
sarahflowers201@gmail.com

Published by Anointed Fire House

Edited by: Anointed Fire House
www.anointedfirehouse.com

Published by: Anointed Fire House
www.anointedfirehouse.com

Photo Credits: Designerjov Photography
www.designerjov.com

ISBN: 978-1-955557-17-7

Dedication

I dedicate this book to my parents, Rick and Mary Flowers.
The ones who trained and raised me by the guidance of the Holy Spirit.

Honor and Acknowledgments

There are so many people who I would like to honor, and these are just a few.

YAHWEH: I first want to honor God. Thank you, God, for loving me when I did not love myself. Thank you for putting people in my life to help cultivate me. Without these people, I would not be who I am today. "Plans fail for the lack of counsel, but with many advisors they succeed" (Proverbs 15:22).

My Parents: I would like to first honor my parents, Rick and Mary Flowers, for introducing me to the greatest love of my life, Jesus Christ. Thank you for your obedience of how to raise and train me up as a child. Thank you for loving me and being my greatest prayer warriors. You both truly raised me up in the love of Jesus Christ. I love you so much. Ephesians 6:4 reads, "And ye fathers, provoke not your children to wrath, but bring them up in the nurture and admonition of the Lord." I'm so thankful to have you both as my parents. You have gone above and beyond what I could have ever asked for.

My Brother: To my big brother, Ricky, who has always taught me to love the beautiful masterpiece God has created in the mirror—ME! You taught me to be a strong warrior and to always remember the mighty God we serve.

Mother Sarah: I was named after a woman named Mother Sarah. She is a woman who ministered to my mom through challenging times in her teenage years. She is a mighty prayer warrior. My mom tells me the love of Christ that she exhibited and still exhibits has changed her life forever, so thank you, Mother Sarah.

My Grandparents: I thank God for both sets of grandparents who instilled the Word of God in me. Please know that God's Word will continue to pass down to all of our generations on both sides of our families.

Grandpa Fox: I'm also thankful for Grandpa Fox who always reminds me to preach the gospel of Jesus Christ, and to continue to keep my knees ashy for the Lord in prayer.

My Spiritual Parents: Apostle Bryan and First Lady Patrice Meadows, my shepherds/pastors who have been raising me in the gospel of Jesus Christ by the guidance of the Holy Spirit. Thank you for being amazing spiritual parents and teaching me the importance of being my authentic self.

Prophetess Joanne Goddard: For your teaching, discipling, instructing and training me in intercession and the prophetic. Prophetess Joanne is the House Prophet of Embassy City. She leads the intercessory prayer and prophetic team.

Elder Tiffany Buckner: For teaching, training, instilling and instructing me on how to love myself and to see myself the way God sees me. Also, for teaching me to use the hands He has blessed me with for His glory, and to always remember the LOVE OF THE FATHER.

Pastor Ajani Brown: For training and guiding me in intercession to be the authentic-self intercessor God has called me to be. Thank you for training me and being a shepherd over the souls of the Kingdom of God by the leading of Holy Spirit.

Embassy City: There are so many people who have instilled a great deal of love and wisdom in me. This church has made me a better person all around. I love my church family, and it's an honor to serve together in the Kingdom of God. Thank you to every partner, leader, intercessor and prophet who has prayed for me.

Ms. Shireen Hunte: For your prayers, guidance and encouragement throughout my life.

To Everyone in My Life: Thank you to every aunt, uncle, cousin, family member, friend, teacher, ICU doctors and anybody who has ever prayed for me privately and publicly.

May the blessing of the Lord be upon you all forever, in Jesus' name.

Table of Contents

Introduction

Do you know that you're an intercessor? Intercession is not just for the old school mother at the church in the back pew, but we are all called to intercession. In order to fully walk in the role of the intercessor God has called you to be, it's important to know that you serve the greatest weapon: Jesus Christ. He is the Great Almighty One who has already fought for us by dying on the cross. He also gives us war strategies in order to annihilate the enemy in our daily lives through scriptures. Throughout my life, God has shown me myself in visions, dreams and trances. I was wearing war gear in several scenarios, destroying the enemy. I never knew what He meant, but He put the pictures together to help me understand the importance of Ephesians 6. When we hear about the armor of God, we sometimes get familiar with the passage since we've learned this in Sunday school. Nevertheless, God literally took the words off the pages and birthed them into real life experiences. It's important for intercessors to know that God uses us as vessels to destroy the works of darkness. Our presence alone makes the enemy nervous because we carry the Spirit of the Lord inside of us. Truly know who you are and the purpose He has called you to complete, because this is what we'll need to destroy the enemy and lead others to Christ. You are powerful. We do not serve a weak God, but one who is omnipotent and omnipresent. We serve an undefeated God! There was a point in my life where I had a vision of myself shaking in my armor when another warrior handed me my sword. The sword represents the Word of God. I was lacking in that area. As warriors, we must sharpen our armor and allow the Lord to complete the inner work in our hearts. How can we defeat the enemy without fully recognizing the power we have? We can appear to have it all together but be so far from God. As warriors, it's important to be honest with the Lord about every area in our lives that we are deficient so we can heal and be set free. The more I surrendered to God and was honest with Him regarding the areas I needed healing, the stronger and sharper my armor became. God wants us to be whole spiritually, physically and mentally. I pray this book sharpens the armor we are supposed to have on daily, and that you encounter the Lord face-to-face in ways you have never experienced. In this book, you'll read some of the encounters that I have experienced. I pray that He comes to you in dreams, visions, trances and face-to-face encounters. If you are not too familiar with trances, Acts 10:10 discusses Peter's trance. It's an encounter you can have by being in two places at once. Throughout my life I have experience supernatural intercession.

After reading Ephesians 6, I pray that you no longer read it the way you used to read it, but God gives you a new perspective, and that you use it in everyday life. It's time for you to arise like never before, WARRIOR!

Prayer:

- ◆ Lord, we thank You for this day. We ask You to open our hearts and ears in ways we have never experienced. We thank

You, Lord, that You have made us weapons of mass destruction for Your glory. Help us to continue to go through this thing called life as You lead the way. Help us to wear our armor daily. God, we release any worry to You and stand firm in Your Word, knowing that it will never return to us void. We thank You that we don't serve a weak God but an atomic bomb of victory. Let us no longer just read Your Word, but let us be doers of the Word. Lord, we are open and ready for new encounters with You. We invite You in every area of our lives. Let there not be any place in our lives that You're absent from Sharpen our armor. We thank You that every enemy has already been destroyed. The battle is not ours but Yours. We decree peace over our minds and hearts. We replace any worry with confidence, knowing that You have already gone before us. Lord, we thank You for being counted as one of Your mighty warriors. We thank You that You are the Author of Peace, and we are heirs. We have Your DNA in our blood, in Jesus' name. Amen.

Chapter 1

Who is an Intercessor?

Pop goes the pop tart out of the toaster. The devil turned into a pop tart right before my eyes. I was about three-years old. He was chasing me in my own home, trying to cause havoc. I was scared and wondered where everybody was at. He was laughing and trying to intimidate me, but after chasing me around the house, he then turned into a pop tart and vanished. This gave me the confidence to know that the devil is powerless. I had the power at the age of three to stop in my tracks and command that devil to flee in the name of Jesus. But if you don't know the power you have and the weapons you carry, he will have a field day in your life. This dream also led me to understand that he was trying to cause chaos in my home. This experience alerted me to intercede for my household. Whatever the enemy was trying to do, God wasn't allowing it. I remember being a little girl and telling my mom the devil turned into a pop tart; we started laughing hysterically. You have to laugh at the enemy because he tries to appear strong, but as children of God, we serve the Great I Am. We are undefeated because He already defeated the enemy. Nothing can stand against our God. As intercessors, we must understand that weapons try to form, but they will not prosper. Our prayers of intercession guards our families, friends, nations, our world and our enemies. The point I want to make is that God speaks to the intercessor in so many ways at any age. God wants you to grow into the intercessor He has called you to be. As intercessors, we can be confident and bold with our prayers. Just like the enemy tried to intimidate me, he tries that with many people. But as intercessors, we are able to step in and use the power that God gives us to stand in the gap and kick the devil out flat on his face.

Always remember the devil is weak and has already been sentenced to the lake of fire. Many times, we make ourselves weapons against ourselves. If you are dealing with anything that is trying to block you from your next dimension of intercession, I decree that you are free today. You're an undefeated champion made by the great King.

Who is an intercessor? An intercessor goes to God concerning His people. As an intercessor, you cover God's people. God uses each of us as agents. Later, in the chapters to come, we will discuss the different types of agents we are as intercessors. You may go to God concerning His people in different ways. Ask the Lord to open up your eyes and ears. Your gift of discernment will guide you to know how to intercede in different situations. Between the ages three and six, the Lord activated my gift of intercession and prophecy. I remember it like it was yesterday. I felt the hurt of a woman. I looked over and saw her in a wheelchair at the grocery store. The Holy Spirit began to speak to me in the aisle concerning her. He said go and speak to that woman. I went over and said, "Do you have any children?" She looked at me and said, "I do have children." I then told her, "Call them. They want to hear from you." She began to cry, and with tears streaming down her face, she said, "They wouldn't want to talk with me." I told her to call them. "They want to hear from you," I reiterated. My mother was watching me from a distance and knew I was being led by the Holy Spirit. The Lord was allowing me to be sensitive so that I could feel her hurt. My prayer to the Lord was that she opened her heart to love again; this was the intercessor in me, but the word of reconciliation with her family was the prophetic word God had me to release. She had to bring her emotions to God, even if they were anger or worry, and she needed to request grace and mercy. This helps to really meet the person where they are at when ministering to them. Many times, as a teenager, my mother would rock me and pray over my womb because intercession and prophetic words would bubble up over me. At this time, I didn't master knowing how to fully navigate this gift. I would have so many words and prayers for people all around me that I could barely stand up. My sensitivity increased to many levels. I could be out with my mom, and the need to intercede and the spirit of prophecy would come on me strong. I wasn't even a teenager yet when we went to a church service and my mom rocked me, because in that moment, God was giving me mail about certain people in the room. He was even having me connect people who I did not know were related.

I realized as an intercessor, you give birth to many of God's promises and plans. At times, you may see an intercessor travail or hold his or her stomach. That is the gift of intercession being activated through the womb. Inside the intercessor's stomach, God is downloading names, ideas, people, situations, etc.

Oftentimes, when you are praying for others, you're a midwife. The intercessor is able to identify the different cries of the people. There are cries of deliverance, war cries, and even the cries of a person giving birth. I command the intercessor in you to arise like never before in this moment!!!

God can show you in several ways how to intercede for people. He may show you in a dream, vision or even give you access to conversations, encounters, etc. He may allow you to feel the hurt and pain that the person feels. People may even reach out to you for prayer. No matter what way God speaks to you, remain sensitive. At times, He may not have released you to speak about what you see and sense in that moment. That's why it's important to have intimacy with the Holy Spirit and make sure you're moving at His beat and pace. When I was a young girl, I smelled the spirit of death when a person walked by me. He wanted me to intercede because some things are not meant to be said. He may show you something, but your assignment is to only pray. The next day, one of the person's family members was murdered. I beat myself up for years thinking I could have stopped what took place, but God had me prepared to pray and intercede for the family and friends who were affected. As intercessors, there will be times when we are called to only intercede in our private time for situations.

There were many times I walked away from my parents to pray for or prophesy over strangers and family members. The intercessors' time clock never ends. In fact, to truly put on the mantle of the intercessor, you break your own biological clock in exchange for His time. He may wake you up in the midnight hour. He may have you pull over and start interceding, or even go into a bathroom stall at work. We are ALL called to be intercessors 24/7 and 365 days of the year. There are so many people who are hurting and need to be reminded that

God is concerned about them. You can be minding your own business when, out of nowhere, you can suddenly feel heavy or depressed. This is the intercessor feeling the hurts of people. God can also allow you to hear the conversations and see the battles people are fighting. As intercessors, we cover people. We are not only called to cover our family and friends, but the whole world. We don't just cover who we want to, but we cover the people God puts on our hearts. One day, you may be praying for one thing, and then He may stop you and have you to pray for our president. If someone calls and asks you to pray for him or her, you're standing in the gap for that person. You're going to the throne room and asking your Savior to intervene for your brother or sister. I remember being a camp counselor, and many of the children were afraid to pray. The ones who did not want to pray ended up loving to pray. I told them prayer is speaking with the heavenly Father; you don't have to sound deep or use big words. Many of the kids who had issues became some of the greatest prayer warriors at that camp. I would tell them that He is their friend and He loves them. I also told them that He would want to hear from them. That is the same for you and me. Many people get intimidated about intercession because they're afraid of praying out loud, or they may not sound a certain way. Remember that you already have a relationship with God through your daily prayer life. As intercessors, when you pray out loud or on behalf of someone else, you're giving onlookers a preview of what you have been doing behind closed doors with the Father. If your prayer time and intimacy is not strong with the Lord, it's never too late to begin. It's okay if you have to start at the beginning. If you need to start praying for five minutes each day, and add on five more minutes every day, you will continue to build on your capability. We have to start somewhere. Challenge yourself to pray each day, adding on more time to your prayer schedule subsequently. Today is a new day for you. Let's get on those knees and get them ashy. He is waiting. He is our Father, and He wants us to come to Him concerning our lives and the lives of others. When you truly surrender to the call of the intercessor, you are able to understand that this is not a natural fight. Ask the Lord to open your spiritual senses so that you can become sensitive in the spirit concerning His people. Life is not a joke, and as intercessors, we must make sure we are fully covered to adequately destroy the works of darkness. We ensure that we are fully covered by wearing our armor 24/7.

Intercessors wear many hats. We are warriors, CIA agents, advocates, watchmen and more, but before we step out, we must know who we are and that we serve the greatest weapon. As intercessors, we must put away the old armor. Your prayers are powerful, intercessor. You are a threat to the enemy's kingdom. No matter how hard it gets through the tests and trials, be strong and keep praying. Even if you have one word to say, Jesus will meet you. Remember the thief on the cross? In Luke 23:42-43, it states, "And he said unto Jesus. Lord, remember me when thou comest into thy kingdom. And Jesus said unto him, verily I say unto thee. Today shalt thou be with me in paradise." Jesus is the best and first example of intercession. Sometimes, the need to intercede comes when you least expect it. Many of my encounters with intercession have been at work, stores, school, etc. You're not always going to be at your bedside interceding, but in the moment of a challenge, press through with the faith you have. Jesus will meet you. Jesus and the thief were in tough situations, but even through the struggles, Jesus answered the thief's cry. It's important to understand that your call to intercession has other people's lives on the line. Jesus could have said, "Are you really about to ask me for help while I'm suffering?"Jesus had blood dripping down His face, and He was about to die, but He still had compassion. Of course, we are not Jesus, but as His children, we should show love to others in the way Holy Spirit leads us. Never think you're too far from God for Him to hear you. Psalms 139:8 states, "If I ascend up into heaven, thou art there: if I make my bed in hell, behold thou art there." No matter where we are, if we call on Him, He will answer. Sometimes, He doesn't answer the way we want, but we must trust Him. Don't stop interceding. You are strong. Even in your weakest moments, He is made strong for you.

Chapter 2

Remove All Funky Armor

Warriors, it's important to remove all gear that God did not put on you. But in order to fight effectively, you must know the gear He wants you to wear and know the importance of each piece. What if a Navy Seal wore the garments of a Marine, and they had an assignment in the water? As warriors, the Word of God gives us instructions regarding what we should be wearing in the spirit as our armor. In Ephesians 6, we are able to identify what we should be wearing.

Looking at 1 Samuel 16:7, we are able to recognize that people see the outer appearance, but God sees the heart. What if you were standing in front of God and He saw your gear in the spirit? Begin to do a self evaluation and look at the gear that you're wearing. Remove all gear that would try to hold you back from fully being the intercessor and warrior God has called you to be. Warriors in a battle of war who carry unnecessary weight on their shoulders tend to tire out quicker, even if they're the strongest in their units because they carry weight that wasn't meant to be there.

A few pieces of the gear that I wore for many years was self-hatred, suicide, depression, fear, low self-esteem and a host of insecurities. Of course, I had to have help removing these garments. I did not like myself for many years. I didn't like my face, my body, my height or my personality. I didn't even like who God created me to be. I couldn't stand looking in the mirror, so I looked for love and acceptance from others. I was eventually able to get the help I needed to truly love everything about myself. As intercessors, we must decide to destroy any demonic interference, even if it's our own personas. If you're not comfortable with yourself or if you're wearing false armor in battle, you won't be as effective as you could have been. But if you get the healing that you need by counseling, mentorship, Godly counsel, deliverance, etc., nothing can stop you. As intercessors, we must evaluate and see what gear is not from God. Sometimes, the traumas in our lives need more attention. The Bible tells us to seek wise counsel. Don't be afraid to get help. Once I decided to remove and clean every piece of gear that smelled funky, I became stronger with how I dealt with life. We should only be wearing the gear that God has us to wear. One of many things that I pray to my Savior is to show me myself. What areas in me are not a sweet aroma in His presence? Having that open communication with the Father is beautiful because you're admitting you need His saving grace.

Surrender, at times, is not enough, but we have to get extra help. Going through deliverance is also a way to address any gear that God did not create. I went through deliverance, counseling, mentorship and received wise counsel for many years. This was one of the best decisions I could ever make for my life. I went as far back as my childhood, and then my intercession went to another dimension. Jesus wants us whole in every area of our lives. Just like warriors train before battle, He wants to make sure our souls are built up in Him. If you look at how the army trains new soldiers, they don't just throw them out, but they train them rigorously.

The more you confess, the more He is able to work on your heart and give you strategies. Do you know that your heavenly Father is undefeated? Do you know the kind of weapons that you have inside of you? The more you spend time with God, the more you will be able to see how gentle and concerned He is about you. I love interceding for others, but one thing I really enjoy is when God shows me myself. I always pray that God shows me areas that I need to work on. I love when God interjects and brings me my own prophetic words about myself. There was a time in my life when I knew an old garment was expiring. He showed me a vision of myself in a prison cell, and then I let out a scream from hell. That's when the black garment suddenly came off and the prison doors flew wide open. The gear that needed to come off was torment. I did not know who I was, so I listened to the enemy's lies. I used to allow him to beat me up so badly with lies and negative words that my head would physically hurt. My past of molestation and rejection would replay in my mind over and over again to the point where I did not know my identity. I was also more concerned about the opinions and lies of the enemy than God's truth. I'm here to tell you today that God's love will drown the enemy's lies if you receive it. 1 John 4:18 states, "There is no fear in love. But perfect love drives out fear, because fear has to do with punishment. The one who fears is not made perfect in love." God has made me all over again. I experienced His love all over again. It's like He continuously dips me in this bath of love. I'm so in love with Him.

To be your own intercessor teaches you how to love and experience the grace that God gives. When He shows you things about yourself, begin to pray for yourself. Ask the Lord to reveal areas that you need healing. Pray over yourself and be sensitive and open. God is concerned about you and wants to heal you. Whatever you need Him to do, open up your mouth and heart and ask Him to come see about you. He cares about you and wants to restore you. I say this to emphasize that God speaks to His children about themselves. Many months to come after this encounter of being released from prison, I went through one of the greatest deliverances of my life. I love when God shows me areas that He wants to work on because it shows how much He cares. God is just like parents who won't give their children dessert for breakfast. The kids wonder why their parents won't let them do what they want them to do, but it's for their good. God watches over us because we are His children. Don't be afraid to let Him to search your heart. Nothing is too hard for God. He makes ALL things work together for our good, according to the book of Romans 8:28.

Ephesians 6:11-18 states, "Put on the whole armor of God, that you may be able to stand against the wiles of the devil. For we wrestle not against flesh and blood but against principalities, against powers, against the rulers of the darkness of this world, against spiritual wickedness in high places. Wherefore take unto you the whole armor of God, that ye may be able to withstand in the evil day, having done all to stand. Stand therefore, having your loins girt about with truth, and having on the breastplate of righteousness. And your feet shod with the preparation of the gospel of peace. Above all, taking the shield of faith, wherewith ye shall be able to quench all the fiery darts the wicked. And take the helmet of salvation, and the sword of the spirit, which is the Word of God. Praying ALWAYS with all prayer and supplication in the spirit and watching thereunto with all perspective and supplication for all saints."

Wearing our armor helps us to function and live daily as intercessors and children of God. We must no longer be hearers of the Word, but doers of the Word when it comes to putting on the full armor of the Lord. Many of us were taught the breakdown of the full armor of God, but let's look at Ephesians 6:11 from a new lens. Let's not just state this scripture, but we must apply it to our everyday lives. Our Bibles are our weapons and GPS. The Bible teaches us how to respond to situations and how to deal with our challenges. James 1:22 states, "But be ye doers of the word, and not hearers only, deceiving your own selves."

Many times, as intercessors, we become tired

easier than most people. There are many factors that can contribute to this, including being out of shape spiritually or trying to fight a spiritual fight with natural weapons. There was a time when a friend of mine was dealing with a demonic spirit, and God allowed me to come face-to-face with it. You would think from my pop tart incident that I would open up my mouth and declare the Word of the Lord. I was still dealing with fear and not realizing the weapons that I had. BAMMMMM! I hit that spirit with my fist, and it didn't flinch. The Holy Spirit spoke to me and said, "Declare the Word of the Lord." Once I addressed the spirit and declared the Word of the Lord, that friend did not deal with that spirit another day.

As intercessors, God will have you travail in the spirit concerning His people. There have been many cases where the Holy Spirit allowed me to have encounters concerning His people in intercession. I remember one time praying with my mother, and I took her hand. As she prayed, I felt my feet scoot across water, and then into somebody's house. He then brought me into a conversation, and it appeared they were worried about a situation. I then understood to pray specific prayers for this person in my time of intercession and also speak to them directly. As intercessors, God wants to take us to places we have never been, and He wants to do this for His glory. God can supernaturally take you to a place and give you insight into situations because you are His intercessor. The more trust you have in the Father, the more He will give you. As agents of God, it is very important for us to spend intimate time with the Lord so we'll be able to download and understand His war strategies against the enemy. The Holy Spirit guides and helps us through life, but how can we fully commune with Him if we don't spend time with Him?

Chapter 3

Armor Activation

Do you remember back in Sunday school when you would walk into the classroom and find out that you were learning about Ephesians 6? When I was young, I was so excited to complete the activities about the armor of the Lord, but I didn't really learn how to truly apply Ephesians 6 as a doer in my everyday life. Let's not just read the scripture, but digest it. Like army soldiers and warriors, when we first enter training, we will receive manuals, but eventually, we have to truly study and know our strategies on the war grounds. As children of God, embracing our gift of intercession and receiving Jesus Christ are the best and first things we did as believers. Accepting Jesus as your Lord and Savior is the most precious and eternal gift you will ever receive. As believers, we must know the importance of our spiritual uniform. What is a helmet in the natural? A helmet protects the brain and the head. It not only protects the head, but it protects the mind. A spiritual helmet does the same thing. Psalms 37:39 states, "The salvation of the righteous is from the Lord; He is their stronghold in the time of trouble." There are benefits of receiving Jesus Christ as your Lord and Savior. Wearing the helmet of salvation represents the citizenship of the Kingdom of God. When you receive Jesus as your Lord and Savior, you're no longer the same man or woman. 2 Corinthians 5:17 states, "Therefore, if anyone is in Christ, he is a new creation. The old has passed away; behold, the new has come." We have to decide to crucify our own flesh. Galatians 5:24 states, "And they that are Christ's have crucified the flesh with the affections and lust." When we receive Jesus as our Lord and Savior, we give up our old habits, mindsets and lifestyles. It's important to protect your mind because, as intercessors, we are very sensitive in the spirit. As intercessors, we have to make sure our gear is sharp because we are God's agents. One of the best things I did when I received Jesus was to relinquish my old thinking patterns. When I decided to put on the mind of Christ, I started living in a state of peace that I could not explain. When we crucify our own flesh, we must crucify our old thinking patterns as well. As intercessors, we are guards and protectors. Don't get distracted by your own self or the enemy. Focus on God and where He is leading you in covering His people. We must be careful regarding what we allow in our minds. The scripture states in Philippians 4:8, "Finally, brethren, whatsoever things are true, whatsoever things are honest, whatsoever things are just, whatsoever things are pure, whatsoever things are lovely, whatsoever things are of good report, if there be any virtue and if there be any praise, think on these things." The reason the scripture states this is because the enemy likes to attack the mind. But since you have received Jesus

Christ, your head is covered and protected; nothing can destroy your mind. The enemy tries to make himself big, but always remember that he is already defeated. Many times, we become our own enemies fighting against ourselves. As warriors, this causes us to be distracted. There is one enemy, and that's the devil. He wants us to lose focus and fight with each other at times. Can you imagine a soldier on the field getting mad at his fellow soldier? That's the perfect time for the enemy or even the enemy of your own mind to get through the cracks. Focus, intercessor. Focus.

The Bible doesn't tell us if we need to put on our gear, but it tells us that we will need it. So, even if thoughts come up with the intent of holding us back, they will fall to the ground because our minds are protected by our heavenly Father. You have to speak over your mind and say, "Let this mind be in me that is in Christ Jesus" (Philippians 2:5). Cover your mind with His Word daily. If you allow the enemy or even yourself to cloud your mind, you won't be able to think straight. If this means you need to go to therapy, to journal, to work out, etc., make sure you do it so you can live in peace. God did not call us to live in confusion or chaos. We serve the Author of peace.

Prayer:

◆ Lord, I thank You for my helmet of salvation. I thank You for sending Your Son, Jesus Christ, to die on the cross for me. I have decided to crucify my own way of thinking. I plead the blood of Jesus over my mind. My mind is whole and full of the wisdom of Christ. I destroy every demonic kingdom that would ever try to come against my mind. I thank You for the power and authority to tread upon scorpions and pythons. Keep my mind stayed on You. I thank You for the peace that surpasses all understanding. Father, You are the

Author of peace, therefore, I can live in it daily. I receive my inheritance of peace everlasting, in Jesus' name. Amen.

The Breastplate of Righteousness

What is a breastplate? What does the breastplate cover? The breastplate covers the spiritual and natural heart of the warrior. What does it look like to wear the breastplate of righteousness in everyday life? In order to walk in righteousness, we must know how to define righteousness. According to Merriam Webster, righteousness is, "Acting in accord with divine or moral law; free from guilt or sin." Don't be afraid of the word righteousness. It's knowing how your heavenly Father wants us to live, and using His Word to give you guidance regarding how to respond to life. In order to make sure you're following Christ, you need to know His commandments and how He wants us to function through His Word. James 5:16 states, "Confess your faults to another, and pray one for another, that ye may be healed. The effectual fervent prayer of a righteous man availeth much." Continue to pray over your heart. God honors those who walk in righteousness.

The scripture states in Psalms 51:10, " Create in me a clean heart, O God; and renew a right spirit within me." Continue to protect and guard your heart. Give no room for the enemy. Jesus was the closet person to God and the humblest person we have ever discovered. Even through the process and until His death on the cross, Jesus made sure He protected His heart as our Chief Intercessor. Even through the beating, rejection, betrayal and the bloodshed,He still managed to get a prayer out on the cross. He could have called down angels from Heaven, but He believed we were that special. Jesus died for us, and did not care about titles or being seen. Jesus did not just say He loved us, but He showed it. We have to get to the point, even through the process of hurt, to trust in the Lord in our hearts and minds. There are so many times when our flesh wants to do the opposite of what God told us to do, but we must subject our hearts to the Lord. Darts of lies, insecurities and so much more will try and tempt your heart into receiving false beliefs. Jesus protected His heart while on the cross. He could have dwelt on the fact that many of the people didn't really love Him. Instead, He decided to pray through it to save us all.

In order to understand what righteousness is, we must open our Bibles and study the scriptures. Jesus was tempted in the wilderness in Matthew 4. He was fasting and praying when the enemy tried to come in three ways, but Jesus stood strong and did not fall into the trap of the enemy. This verse helps us to understand the importance of fasting and protecting how we respond to life. There have been so many times when God has brought me revelation through fasting. Consequently, I had better responses to situations. As an intercessor, it's important to make fasting a regular strategy. Life gets hard, and there are many times when we are tempted by evil, but fasting gives us the strength to resist the enemy and discipline our souls. As a child, I would hear people say I wouldn't want to become a Christian because it's boring. But God doesn't want us to follow His commandments to live boring lives. He wants to protect us like a mother and father protects their young. Jesus knows the consequences of sin, and gives us a way out of it. Sin may feel fun for a little while, but the scripture states in Romans 6:23, "The wages of sin is death but the gift of God is eternal life." When you start growing closer to God, you learn that He is more fun than anything else. In the times where I did fall short of God's glory, the sin had been fun for a while, but afterwards, I felt empty. Begin to study how Jesus responds to people in the Bible in situations and even parables. Righteousness is not about being perfect, but living a life submitted to God and knowing His grace will carry you. God never intended us to be perfect, and that's why He sent us a Savior. In John 8, people wanted to throw stones at a woman for falling into sin, but Jesus stepped in. There is blood for us when we fall. Oftentimes, people will pick on others because their sins were made public. When Jesus stepped in and stopped them from stoning the woman, it shows the grace He has for us all. Nobody is perfect, and we have all fallen short of the glory. Thank God for sending the Deliverer, Jesus Christ. Ask the Lord to help you in your decisions and to protect your heart. It's so important to do a heart scan. As intercessors, God shows us so much, but never think you don't need to check your heart.

As intercessors, we are protectors and we must be sensitive, even with the conversations we have. There have been many cases where I have left rooms because of the conversations that were taking place. We must protect our senses in the spirit. God may want you to pray for that person, but you allowed negative conversations to get into your ear gates. Ask God to make you more aware and sensitive to His Spirit. I pray often for the Lord to make my heart like His. Protect what comes into your heart; this includes words and people. If anyone starts talking badly about someone, end the conversation immediately or challenge that person to pray for the individual he or she is speaking reproachfully about for at least sixty minutes. There are so many things that God wants to show His people, but how can we hear Him if we are gossiping or speaking badly about others? Protect your ear gates. Gossip is like poison to the intercessor. My sensitivity to conversations has grown stronger and stronger since I was a little child. My mother was a great example of an intercessor. My parents taught me to love and not talk ill about people. I never heard my parents talk badly about someone. Request that the Lord be in the conversations that you have and in everything that you do. Genesis 1:26 states, "We are made in the image of God." When you're having conversations, always remember that you are a representative of Jesus Christ. Anoint your tongue and mouth, and pray over them. As intercessors, we have no time to poison our mouths with filth. When you allow filth into your mind, it then gets into your heart and spirit. Proverbs 4:23, "Above all else, guard your heart, for everything you do flows from it." There is a reason we must protect our hearts, especially on the battlefield. How can we function fully as His soldiers if we don't know who He is and we don't have His fruits? Oftentimes, the soldiers in war move by the direction of their sergeants. We must move at the Lord's rhythm, including His heartbeat. Often, we hear people saying, "Lord, I want to be like you," but do we really? When was the last time you prayed for someone you didn't like or someone who betrayed you? When was the last time you paid a waiter a large tip, even though he or she didn't deserve it? If some of us were put in Jesus Christ's shoes, we would have said, "I'm not dying for you guys! So, you're going to love me one minute, then crucify me the next?" But Jesus' heart was already made up that He was going to do what God sent Him down to Earth to do, and that was to save God's people. Jesus did not tolerate negative thoughts that came into His mind. He could have gotten caught up in His feelings and said, "They don't love me. Why should I love them?" But that's where we can see in His character, love and compassion for us.

When I was a young girl, I remember there was a woman who would give my mom a hard time at work. I drew a picture and told my mom to give it to the lady. At a young age, God gave me the sensitivity to know how to operate in His love, even through hardened hearts. I haven't been perfect. There have been several times the Holy Spirit has given me a rebuke. The times I have failed in guarding my heart or even my ear gates, I repented and asked God to close any demonic doors that I allowed to open. Thank God for grace and repentance; we all need it.

Prayer:

◆ As I cover my heart with my hand, I ask You, Lord, to protect my heart. Guard my heart from anything that is not pleasing to You. I repent for any time I allowed filth to enter my heart and mind. Let me have Your heart and let me desire what You desire for me. Remove anything from my heart that needs to be left at Your cross. Heal my heart from any brokenness, wounds or unresolved heartbreaks. Do spiritual surgery on my heart and make me over again. Lord, show me, in my words and actions, how to love people. Show me the areas I need to help in to truly be whole in You. Give me a desire to walk in Your character and not my own selfish attitude. Open my eyes and ears to study Your character and truly walk in

Your image. Help me to forgive and pray for all people, in Jesus' name. Amen.

The Sword of the Spirit

As an intercessor, making sure your sword is sharpened is imperative. Do not allow your sword to become rusty. I charge you today to make sure you're in your Word daily. Warrior, the Word of God makes the enemy disintegrate when he tries to rise. Your sword allows you to be reminded of what God has already said. It not only gives you power over the enemy, but it gives you direction regarding how to live as a Christian. You train by being in your Word daily. We must spend time in our Word just like we need nutrition in our physical bodies. If we do not eat the Word, we are weak soldiers. We serve such a powerful God that anything you face already know that you are more than a conqueror, according to Romans 8:37. Make sure you protect what you let in your mind. There are scriptures for every situation that we go through. Don't get so familiar with the Word that you forget to use it in life's situations. If you're dealing with doubt, you can go to Matthew 21:22. It reads, "And whatever you ask in prayer, you will receive, if you have faith." If you're dealing with anger, you can pull up Ephesians 4:26; it states, "Be angry and do not sin; do not let the sun go down on your anger." If you're dealing with sickness in your body, the scripture says in Isaiah 53:5, "By His stripes we are healed." Normalize reading and studying the scriptures so that when situations arise, they will naturally come up in your spirit as your response. As I look back over my life, I realize I missed the mark by not allowing the Word to be my first response to situations and challenges. You will save yourself heartache and pain by responding to life's situations in accordance with how the scripture tells us to respond. If you're in a difficult situation, and a scripture does not come to mind that corresponds with that particular situation, Google it or even buy a Strong's Concordance. The Word of God states in Hebrews 4:12, "For

the Word of God is quick, and powerful and
sharper than any two edges sword, piercing
even to the dividing asunder of soul and spirit,
and of the joints and marrow, and is a
discerner of the thoughts and intents of the
heart." When the Bible tells us about the
sword, it means the Word of God. There have
been many situations in my life where I
responded first out of my flesh and did not pick
up my Bible. Studying scripture will allow you
to be ahead of the enemy. You will end up
having peace that surpasses understanding. In
situations whereby you are are feeling
impatient, remember Sarah in Genesis 16. If
you find yourself frustrated and in need of
healing, remember the man in the book of John
who was at the pool of Bethesda. The angel of
the Lord troubled the waters, but he did not
have strength to get into the pool on his own.
Jesus found him where he was and healed
him. If you find yourself in need of peace,
remember when Jesus spoke to the storm and
said, "Peace, be still" in the book of Mark. At

times, we read the Word so many times and forget to apply it to our lives. If the enemy tries to make you feel condemned, you can tell that devil to SHUT UP! The Word says in Romans 8, "There is therefore now no condemnation to them which are in Christ Jesus, who walk not after the flesh but after the Spirit." As soldiers in the army of the Lord, having the Word in your spirit is important. This is because, as intercessors, we sometimes have to carry others on the field while we are dealing with our own situations in life. When people call you to pray, there should be a scripture that opens up in your spirit to be released.

Prayer:

◆ Lord, I thank You for the Word that gives me direction regarding how to respond in life. Lord, give me a desire to be in Your Word. Help me to use Your Word daily, even in life's situations. Let Your Word go before me. Help me to study Your Word daily. I repent for anytime I acted in accordance with my flesh and not Your Word. Make me over again. Let me always go to Your Word regarding how to deal with situations and allow the Holy Spirit to guide me. Help me, Lord; I need it. Give me a desire to be in Your Word daily. Give me a desire to use Your Word in every area of my life. Build me up and tear down any words that are contrary to Your Word that I have allowed in my life. Let Your Word guide me into all truth, in Jesus' name. Amen.

Gospel of Peace

Intercessor, don't forget the importance of knowing that from the top of your head to the bottom of your feet, the anointing flows. The Gospel of Peace is located on your feet because it's important to always spread the gospel of Jesus Christ wherever you go. Don't go through life without spreading the gospel. As warriors, we serve a God who is Prince of Peace. We can live in peace everyday by spreading the gospel of Jesus Christ. We have the right to live in peace daily. My goal is to lead at least 300 million souls to Christ before the coming of the Lord. Make sure you have set goals for leading souls because Jesus Christ is coming back again. As intercessors, make sure that you're asking God to give you opportunities to lead souls to Christ at work, school, grocery stores or wherever your feet should tread. Tell people of the goodness of Jesus and how He saved you. Also tell them that receiving salvation is the greatest decision they could ever make. I remember as a little girl when we moved into a new neighborhood, my mom had me knock on every door in our new neighborhood to see if they had a child my age to play with. I remember being so embarrassed, but this made me bold. I remember the Lord telling me to witness to a neighbor when I was about 12-years old. Sometimes, you don't understand why your parents tell you to do things, but it's all a part of the process of becoming the best version of yourself. Even though I cried and was so frustrated with my mom, I learned so much that day. Do not be afraid to speak and lead souls to Christ. I remember scheduling different days to go over her house and walk her through the process. There are many people who you will witness to that may not come to church, but your life will still serve as an example to them. You may be the only church they see. Make sure you are producing good fruit. Let your lifestyle be an example. People are watching you more than you know. They are watching your conversations and how you respond to situations. There were so many times I responded in faith and not my flesh, and my coworkers would come up to me and ask me why I had so much peace. When people ask you those types of questions, it gives you an opportunity to witness to them. Spreading the good news of Jesus Christ is one of the best things you could ever do because you are growing the army of the Lord. Make sure you're writing sermons on how to receive salvation, and list a few points to give people after they receive Jesus. Some people will receive Jesus, but will not be too sure of what to do after salvation. If you give them guidance and tools, this will help them forever. I challenge you to write sermons of salvation so you can always be ready. At any time, you can introduce and be a witness to someone. We all have a responsibility to lead souls to Christ. I did not like what my mom had me do as far as knocking on doors, but I did find friends and I became confident in leading souls to Christ. Intercessors, it's crucial to make sure that as you're leading others to Christ , Jesus truly knows who you are. You can pray Heaven down, but if He does not truly know you, you won't reap the benefits of salvation. Jesus wants an intimate relationship with you. The Word says in Matthew 7:21-23, "Not everyone who says to Me, Lord Lord, shall enter the kingdom of heaven, but he who does the will of my Father in heaven. Many will say to me in that day, 'Lord, Lord, have we not prophesied in your name, cast out demons in your name, and done many wonders in your name?' And then I will declare to them, I never knew you; depart from Me, you who practice lawlessness!" Make sure you know the Lord and He knows you. Seek Him daily, and lead all the souls to Christ that you can. In order for Him to know you, you have to be made in His image. Repent and turn from evil. Get the help that you need. I did it and I feel 100,000 times lighter!!

Prayer:

♦ Lord, wherever I go, let me spread and testify of the goodness of Jesus Christ. Anoint me from the top of my head to the bottom of my feet. Give me the fire and desire to lead as many souls to Christ before Your second coming. Lord, I want You to truly know me inside out. Lord, dip me in Your love all over again. I repent for my iniquity. Give me the wisdom on how to witness to people.

Lord, I thank You that I can live in peace daily. Let me sit back and enjoy Your peace. Anoint my feet with the fire of the Holy Ghost so that I can spread Your goodness and mercies. Let me have a burning fire and passion to do Your will and be about your business. Help me to plow through this thing called life, and give me the strength I need to stand, even when the pressures of life come upon me, in Jesus' name. Amen.

Shield of Faith

As intercessors, it's important for us to make sure that our faith is fully activated at all times. The enemy and life's situations will try to get us off track. Can you imagine taking your shield off and running onto a war field with arrows coming towards you? We must make sure our shields are up and secure, even in the hardest situations. There were so many times in my life when I put my shield of faith down. Hebrews 11:1 states, "Faith is the substance of things hoped for and the evidence of things not seen." We serve a God who will split the Red Sea on our behalf. Our faith goes beyond what we can comprehend. In the moments when our faith is tested, we automatically want to respond with our flesh. Next time a situation arises, immediately imagine yourself putting up your shield of faith and decreeing the Word of the Lord. Do you remember the war movies and how they would use their shields to protect each other? Leave no open holes where the enemy or doubt can come in. Intercessors are very sensitive; we can pick up on the emotions of others. Your shield of faith is not only used for yourself, but those around you and the territories that you are called to. God gives intercessors different territories and assignments. If there is a certain situation happening in your family or in the world in general, you have the opportunity to use your shield of faith and carry others. For example, from 2020-2021, the world has been dealing with COVID-19. You can put your shield of faith

47

up and decree and declare that no matter what it looks like, things are going to turn around. It's so hard right now because so many people have suffered losses because of this virus. I have lost some family members. As intercessors, let us arise like never before and stand as examples through the struggles of life. Even though COVID has had an effect on the world, we must continue to pray and intercede for our nation. If someone sounds hopeless and fearful, that is an opportunity to release faith in the atmosphere. You can pick certain times of the day to pray against the effects of COVID-19 and continue to use your shield of faith. It's very important to protect your shield of faith because people can cause your faith to deplete. Make sure you're surrounding yourself with people who are carriers of faith. Always protect your thoughts and eliminate doubt. Increase your faith and believe God can do the incredible for you. Let's look at our brother, Noah. Noah began to build an ark because he knew a storm was coming. Do you know how much faith in God he had to have? There were people who didn't believe in him, and they laughed at him. If Noah would have believed them, his faith would have decreased, but since his faith was in God, he had rambunctious faith. There are so many doors of opportunity that open when you allow faith to take root. There are so many ideas inside of you. Refuse to allow the gifts and talents God put inside of you to go barren. I speak to every gift and talent in you, and I decree that you will use what God has put inside of you for His glory. Don't get me wrong—there are times when faith seems impossible, but faith the size of a mustard seed does bear fruit, according to Matthew 17:20. There are times when you just want to give up, but remember the shield you have. You may not have the words to say, but pick up your shield. Refuse to allow the enemy to throw you off your equilibrium. We are the ones to throw him off balance. Anytime he tries to throw arrows your way, open your mouth and command the devil to flee or command that situation to line up with the Word of God. You are a mighty weapon. If God Himself has to split the sea or have you walk on water, believe that He can do it. There are times when our faith is tested. You may even be in a test right now. Go to the mirror and put up your shield of faith, and then decree and declare that God will work on your behalf, in Jesus' name.

When I was a little child, my parents and I experienced a tough situation. We lost our house and cars, so we had to live in a hotel. We also did not have much food. Nevertheless, we were very happy and we grew closer to one another, even through this hard time. There are so many situations that take place in life, but it's how you respond to them that determines the outcome. I remember my parents still worshiping and giving God glory through this situation. I shared a bed with my mom, and my brother shared a bed with my dad. This was one of the best times of my life with my family.

Even through the hardest situations, God will bring glory out of them. No matter where you are at in your life, God hears your cries and He will make all things work together for your good (see Romans 8:28). Life is not easy, but God will walk with you every step of the way. Be encouraged because this is not the final destination. Faith will have you destroying every ounce of pride in your life. My parents taught me the importance of faith in every situation of our lives. I remember when we lost our car, and my dad would ride my bike to the grocery store. My father and mother are worshipers. I always remember them worshiping the Lord, no matter how hard their situations were, even through the tears and pain. There was a point after losing everything that my dad fell on the floor and started crying out to the Lord. Being desperate for Christ, especially in hard times, grows your intimacy because your faith is being tested. God wants us to freely love Him, even when it gets hard. I remember when we didn't have much food and my mom would give my brother and I the last of the potatoes to eat. I'm so thankful for the friends and family who helped us through this time. The values my parents instilled in me of prayer and worship, even through the hardest times, has stayed with me up until now and will stay with me for the rest of my life. Believe that God is not going to leave you where you are at. I remember my family eating together, playing games with each other and serving the Lord in His house during the tests and trials. The tests and trials get rough, but they bring forth a better you. Don't give up! John 13:7 states, "Jesus replied, 'You do not realize now what I am doing, but later you will understand.'" You may be asking God so many questions and wondering why things are going the way they are, and that is okay. Just don't allow your questions to deplete your trust and faith in God. Let your faith be louder!

1 Peter 1:7 states, "These trials are only to test your faith, to see whether or not it is strong and

pure. It is being tested as fire tests gold and purifies it and your faith is far more precious to God than mere gold; so if your faith remains strong after being tried in the test tube of fiery trials, it will bring you much praise and glory and honor on the day of His return." The world is going through so many tests and trials, but be that light that they need by standing on the foundation of faith. Times get so hard, and you may want to give up, but PUSHHHHH!!!!!!! I'm cheering for you!!

Prayer:

◆ Lord, I believe that You can do the incredible. There is nothing too hard for You. Your Word says in Matthew 17:20, "Because you have so little faith. Truly I tell you, if you have faith as small as a mustard seed you can say to this mountain, 'Move from here to there,' and it will move. Nothing will be impossible for you." Lord, I speak to every situation and declare the Word of the Lord over them. I know that You will provide for me and Your people. When my faith is tested, I trust You, Lord, to help me through. Lord, it gets so hard sometimes, but You are the lifter of my head. Lord, help me, in Jesus' name. Amen.

Belt of Truth

We serve the Great I Am. The Word says in John 4:23, "But the hour is coming, and now is when, the true worshipers will worship the Father in spirit and truth; for the Father is seeking such to worship Him. God is Spirit, and those who worship Him must worship Him in spirit and truth." We hold so much power within us because we have the Holy Spirit. There have been many times the enemy would try to play mind games with me, but then the Holy Spirit would lead me back to what the Word says. The Word of God tells us the truth. At times, lies or words contrary to God's Word try to come into our hearts, but that's why we have

God's Word, which is the truth. I remember growing up and dealing with the spirit of rejection majorly. In order for me to know who I was, I had to grow closer to the Father. I always thought I was too different and I never fit in, but the Word says in Peter 2;9, "But ye are a chosen generation, a royal priesthood, an holy nation, a peculiar people; that ye should shew forth the praises of Him who hath called you out of darkness into His marvelous light." When I read this, I began to see that God has created me the way He wanted me to be. I used to hate myself so much because I fed into the lies of the enemy. God wants us to be healthy intercessors in every area of our lives. I remember one night, I was dealing with so much mental warfare when the Lord revealed Himself to me face-to-face in a vision. He had His arms wide open under a sunrise. God will meet you where you're at. I often wonder as to why He didn't visit me when I was walking on glory clouds of peace, but He met me in my struggle. Peace came over my mind so strongly. When I saw Him, I was reminded of His truth. Addressing every door that would stop us from being mighty intercessors lifts so much weight off us. Intercessors, it's so important to know the truth because as you cover the nations, your families, churches, pastors, etc., you're able to cover them with God's truth. Think about it. I can now see clearly because I have broken every lens of distraction and all of the enemy's lies by the blood of Jesus. I decided I would face everything that would try to stop me from being who I am called to be. Once I decided to address every lie and replace it with truth, I have had more encounters with God that have changed my life. It's important to study the Word every day. 2 Timothy 2:15 says, "Study to shew thyself approved unto God, a workman that needed not be ashamed, rightly dividing the word of truth." When you study the Word, you're able to immediately cut through the lies of the enemy with the sword of truth. If you or someone deals with low self-esteem or any negative situation in life, you're able to pray for the truth over those issues by the Word of God. If someone calls you and says that he or she is defeated, raise your sword and release God's truth. In order to fully protect ourselves and others, we must know the truth through His Word. Do not allow the enemy to beat you up in your mind. You are strong, and you are a child of God. You are a mighty warrior for God's Kingdom. Whenever you feel like you're drowning, remember Isaiah 59:19, which reads, "So shall they fear the name of the Lord from the west, and His glory from the rising of the sun. When the enemy shall come in like a flood, the Spirit of the Lord shall lift up a standard against him." I remember a vision I had some time ago. I was in the water, and I felt like I was about to drown. That's when the Spirit of the Lord told me not to be afraid, and He lifted me above the wave. The wave was several feet high. God will help you through your hardships and even through the warfare. Stay calm, warrior, and remember the bullets of

His Word.

Prayer:

◆ Dear Lord, today we shoot down every lie of the enemy that has been spoken over our lives. We decree that we will only speak life and Your truth out of our mouths. Lord, thank You that Your Word is truth. Thank You that we can dwell on Your Word. We break every evil word or curse that has ever been spoken against us, and we plead the blood of Jesus over our lives. Lord, we dwell on what You think and say about us. Lord, we have decided to dethrone every word that is contrary to Your truth. Let us walk in Your truth in all that we do. Heal our land, in Jesus' name. Amen.

Chapter 4

Agents

Agents are representatives. Dear intercessor, we are representatives of Jesus Christ. Jesus uses us in many ways to intercede for the nations. Anytime you are ministering or even going to work, you are being a representative of Jesus Christ. In everything we do and say, we are representatives of Jesus Christ. There are several ways that God uses us as agents We are going to discuss how God uses us as CIA agents, advocates, watchmen and warriors.

CIA stands for Central Intelligence Agency. According to Merriam- Webster, CIA agents are "organized activity of an intelligence service designed to block an enemy's sources of information, to deceive the enemy, to prevent sabotage and to gather political and military information. It's the government organization in the United States that collects secret information about other countries."

Intercessors, do you know that there are secrets that God wants to reveal to us in ways that we could never imagine? You are God's agents for His people. Mighty intercessor, your intercession can unlock codes and crack cases in the spirit. Imagine a trial in the natural. We are agents that can go to the courts of Heaven and try cases concerning God's people and situations. I remember God giving me a vision of a courtroom with files. On the files, there were names with situations. As intercessors, God gives us different people and situations to pray for. I instantly started praying for those people and the different cases in the heavens. There are times when the cases are open and obvious, and there will be times when God tells us the outcome Himself. This is not the time to gossip, but to get on your knees and pray. If the Holy Spirit leads you to do anything else, be sensitive to Holy Spirit. Gossip should make you puke. If you find yourself struggling with gossip, ask the Lord to deliver your tongue. Our God can deliver us from anything. CIA agents are found trustworthy, and not just anybody can be one. Why would God want to give us secrets if we are hurting our brothers and sisters with our words, both openly and privately? Thank God for the blood and His grace! There is repentance for everyone. As CIA agents, God will give you access to realms in the spirit you could never imagine. I decree that God will unlock and reveal codes and cases to you for His glory like never before.

CIA agents are often put in ranks. The more training and years you're in the military, the more access you'll have. In the case of the intercessor, it's called trust. It doesn't matter how long you have been saved. Never think that because you have been saved for 45 years that you have more access. Apostle Paul was called by God when he was involved in killing Christians. He didn't even have time to sit down and get himself "ready." God knew when it was time for Apostle Paul to answer the call. Don't allow the spirit of religion to take over. God will call anyone at anytime. Apostle Paul went from killing Christians to being one of the greatest apostles of all time. Make sure you're spending time with the Lord and allowing the Holy Spirit to guide you. In the chapter to come, we will discuss the importance of the Holy Spirit. God is ready to release codes and secrets like never before, especially in this hour. Make sure you're spending time with the Lord and you're having an intimate relationship with Him. Make up in your mind that you no longer want to date God in intercession, but marry Him.

At times, God has a funny way of showing us His power. My vehicle was in the shop for about three months because they could not figure out what was wrong with the car. Finally,

I became tired of waiting and I declared in that moment that every code would go off to tell these workers the issue with my car. In that moment while I was praying for God to reveal the codes, I received a call that my car randomly stopped while it was in the middle of testing, and many codes went off. They were able to figure out the issue with my vehicle. After this, I was able to see the power of God manifest right before me. There are so many codes and secrets that God can reveal. You have the power in intercession to ask the Lord to reveal the plots and schemes of the enemy. God will get very detailed if you ask Him.

Agents are also spies. There are so many war tactics in the Bible where God used spies. Numbers 13:17 states, "Moses sent them to spy out the land of Canaan and said to them, 'Go up into the Negeb and go up into the hill country.'" Moses sent 12 spies. I pray that every one of us is in a position where God can give us war tactics in the spirit so that we can be ahead of the enemy. Ask the Lord to make you a pure vessel. Tell Him to purify all of your senses in the spirit. We want our smell, sight, touch, taste and hearing to all be clear and pure in the spirit.

As intercessors, we are not only agents but spies in the spirit for the Kingdom of God. We are vessels used to help protect the borders. Ask the Lord to make you a spy in the way of prayer for your family, friends, churches, state and nation. My church has training in both intercession and the prophetic. Build teams in your church so there will be agents all over the body of Christ. Intercessors, there are so many conversations God has given me access to. He wants to reveal so much to you. He has given me so much insight to the point where I was able to identify the exact clothes a person would be wearing and the topic. God can use us to cover the Kingdom of God. There are times when God will allow me to hear conversations about situations people are (or were) going through. I remember a time when God gave me a vision of a conversation somebody typed up where that person had stated that she was struggling with keeping joy and peace. I remember encouraging her and I remember her telling me that what I'd spoken was the exact thing she had been struggling with. There was a time when the Lord showed me a maze. The maze suddenly started shaking like a clock concerning a person. God then revealed to me that the old patterns and negative cycles of thinking were now broken off this person. 2 Kings 6:12 states, "And one of his servants said, None, my lord, O king: but Elisha, the prophet that is in Israel, telleth the king of Israel the words that thou speakest in thy bedchamber."

We can build teams in our churches that will overflow outside and grow the army all over the world. The intercessory prayer team at my church prays before service. Once you ask the chain of command to start an intercessory prayer team, begin to pray for your pastors, family, friends, the entire congregation and the nations. Seek the Lord for prayer points. If you're not sure how to build a team, pick a day out of the week for those who would like to be a part of the team. Assign leadership roles. The scripture states in Matthew 18:20, "For where two or three are gathered together in my name, there I am in the midst of them." Once you all meet up, train up warriors by teaching them the art of intercession. You may have a day when you pray for the nation for thirty minutes, and then have a 15-minute teaching on the topic of intercession. Or you may all just lay prostrate before the Lord, declaring healing for your city.

Allow the Holy Spirit to lead you. It's time for intercessors to arise like never before with wise war tactics to destroy the enemy and cover God's people. If it happens that you are the first and only member of the intercessory prayer team, pray like there are about one million warriors in the room. Remember Gideon in Judges 7? He won the battle over the Midianites. God used him to defeat about 135,000 Midianites with 300 trumpets and men. It doesn't matter if you start with two agents. Judges 7:20, states, "And the three companies blew the trumpets, and brake the pitchers, and held the lamps in their left hands, and the trumpets in their right hands to blow withal; and they cried, the sword of the Lord, and of Gideon." Even in your war cry, there is power. You may only have one word to say, or you may not have any words to say, however, don't neglect to let out a travail and Jesus will meet you. Even your cry has power. Psalms 145:19 states, "He fulfills the desire of those who fear him; he also hears their cry and saves them." Agents arise and spy the land for the Kingdom of God.

Advocates

Every time God gives us an assignment or we receive a prayer request, this reveals that we are advocates. According to Merriam Webster, an advocate is, "one who pleads the cause of another before a tribunal or judicial court." I have had encounters with the Lord where He has taken me to His throne room. But when I looked over, I was bringing someone with me. We are literally God's spokesmen. There are people who don't think they can speak up, and when you have the opportunity to pray for them, be sure to remind them of the power they have. God will give you access to stand in the gap for others; He will even give you access to their case files to ensure that they are taken care of.

There are times when we won't have words to say, and as intercessors, we have the power in our touch to hold and pray over people. Have you ever been rocked by a church mother back in the day? Sometimes, she would just pray or speak in tongues. Depending on the situation, someone needs you to just be there and not say a word. The Holy Spirit will lead you. Sometimes, God wants us to just sit in His presence. From there, He wants us to be quiet and listen for His instruction.

When I was about 16-years old, I went to a church function and I saw a person crying. The tears were flowing, and I did not know what exactly to say. The Spirit of the Lord just told me to hold that person's hand and let her cry. After that day, the person reached out to me to express that she really appreciated that moment. That whole day, I beat myself up and thought I should have said more or even spoke in hard tongues. This is a great example of the importance of allowing the Holy Spirit to lead you. There were so many times I was able to go and witness to people, and in many of those cases, I had no words to say. Sometimes, you just have to let the Holy Spirit fill the room, while you hold the person and encourage them.

As advocates, we speak on behalf of the people. When you're interceding for people, God has given you the dominion power to break muzzles in the spirit. Some people are muzzled by lies and a multitude of fears, but as intercessors, we are able to pray and plead the blood of Jesus so that they can be set free.

There are not many things that upset me, but if you are around me long enough, you would discover that bullying is something that breaks my heart. I dealt with bullying throughout my life. Once I realized the power I had within, I was delivered from timidity. I had to address this spirit of fear and timidity that would try and follow me. I used to be so mad because it was like this bullying spirit had been following me around ever since I was a little girl. 2

Corinthians 10:4 reads, "For the weapons of our warfare are not carnal but mighty through God to the pulling down of strong holds." I realized that the enemy tries to target you even at a young age. He likes to target you because of the anointing and power that is inside of you. That's why it's important to constantly declare and decree the Word of the Lord over your children. My parents constantly spoke the Word over my brother and I, and had us repeat it. We have family videos of my parents having us repeat the Word of God. The thing about me is I did not really believe what I was saying. I only would repeat it. Until I got sick and tired of dealing with the spirit of fear and intimidation, I dealt with the same situations with different people. That's when I finally started to believe God's Word. I dealt with being bullied as a child, and even as I began to grow up. There was a time when the enemy tricked me into believing he had the power. This is when I was being bullied so badly that I was afraid to speak up. I was allowing people to bully me, and that spirit of control was manifesting through them right before my eyes, so much so that I ran and prayed for God to send help in the form of another believer. I found that person, and she took me to a back room and prayed over me. I was being harassed and picked on. When I came home, I ran upstairs to my room and I locked the bathroom door. My mom was an advocate for me. As she banged on the door, I became even more fearful because it sounded like the enemy trying to come after me. The enemy is weak; never forget that. He tries to appear stronger than he is, but the Word confirms that he has already been defeated. My mom would not stop beating on the door until I opened it. Once I opened the door, she had me open my mouth and address that spirit by the power of God. Both my mom and the person who prayed for me were my advocates. They not only prayed over me, but I learned the importance of opening up my own mouth and recognizing the power that I have from the Lord.

Never limit your intercession to a place. There could be a person the Lord leads you to intercede for at work, church, college, etc. These encounters allowed me to see that there was something in me that the enemy did not want me to see. He knows that I am a child of God and I hold power within me. Those two incidents happened weeks apart from one another, and I was able to speak up and address the spirit of fear. Once I addressed it, I did not deal with it again. Never be afraid to open up your mouth and rebuke the devil out of every area of your life.

There are people who are being bullied by the enemy, and as intercessors, we are vessels commissioned to lead them right back to the Father and His truth. If I did not have those advocates to remind me of the power that I already had, I would have stayed in that fear. It's so important to understand the weapons and truth we have in Christ Jesus. There are people who are hurting and living in fear, and they need you to be obedient to the call of intercession. You never know what somebody is going through. You will have many opportunities to intercede when you go to the mall, store, work, college and even when you're talking with a customer service rep over the phone. Make sure that you are intercessors who are loving. Be careful how you treat the waitress and the customer service representative. They could be people God has commissioned you to pray for or minister to, no matter how frustrated you could be with them. There have been times I had to ask the Holy Spirit to help me over the phone. I would pray in that moment and end up praying for or talking about the Lord with the person I was engaging. Never miss an opportunity to witness to someone, no matter where you go. If you are single and want to test the patience of your potential mate, pay attention to how he or she treats the customer service rep over the phone. Help us, Lord!!

As advocates, we stand up and fight for those who aren't able to fight for themselves. The time I locked myself in the bathroom is a perfect example. My mom banged on the door and cast that spirit of fear out of me! I would have been lost in that moment if she hadn't intervened. Intercessors are teachers. When we pray, we teach others what to do so they are able to pray for themselves and do whatever they need to do on their own.

When I was in high school, there was a child with special needs who was being bullied by two boys. I ended up yelling at the bullies, and I told them to leave him alone. There are times when you will have to open up your mouth and command the enemy to get off your family, your friends, your stuff, etc. Looking back I could have told the boys to leave the child alone in a nicer way. As intercessors, something that we could do to end bullying is to advocate for inclusion of mandatory anti-bullying classes in the curriculum. These classes would help so much. Your gift of intercession can be used on all of the seven mountains of influence. The seven mountains of influence are:

- ◆ Education
- ◆ Business
- ◆ Media
- ◆ Entertainment
- ◆ Government
- ◆ Families
- ◆ Religion

As intercessors, we should be praying over these mountains daily. We can bring intercession to each of these mountains. Using my aforementioned example, when praying over the mountain of Education, we can ask God to show us how to build a mandatory curriculum for students that directly addresses bullying.

In college, I changed my major many times. I graduated with a degree in Gerontology. For those who don't know what Gerontology is, it is the study of aging. This major allows you to stand up for older adults. In order to graduate with this major, I was required to complete internship hours. I completed some of my hours at the Ohio Department of Aging. This experience gave me a real life example of the importance of speaking up for others and knowing how to make a change. Many of the older adults that I was able to interview and form projects with allowed me to see the struggles they are faced with while enduring the aging process.

We are advocates in more ways than you think!

Watchman

Have you ever noticed that in the war movies, they would have towers that the soldiers stood on, and those soldiers would be on call 24/7 at different times of the day? Intercessors, we are watchmen for the Kingdom of God. That's why there are different watch hours for each person. God speaks to us all at different intervals throughout the day. Make sure you know your watch hours. There are about eight watch hours. Ever since I was about 16-years old, I have woken up at about three o'clock every morning. I have had to repent because, to be honest, I would go and eat or go right back to sleep. It's so important to get up and pray when the Lord awakens you. You never know what He would have you pray for in that very moment. There have been many times when I would pray for people and not even know who they were. There were even times when I ended up seeing them in real life months later. Your intercession covers and even saves people from car accidents, assaults, etc. You're not only on watch for your family and friends, but the nation, churches and the whole world. Matthew 26:40, states, "Then He returned to His disciples and found them sleeping. Couldn't you men keep watch with me for on hour?" He asked Peter. I remember a time when a person i knew was missing and in danger (I knew the person, but it was not on the news). I commanded the angels of Heaven to arrest the soul of that individual, and hours later, the person was found. Open your mouth, intercessor!! You have Holy Ghost power!

At times, the Spirit of the Lord will wake you up, and you may not have the words to say, but Romans 8:26-27 states, "In the same way, the Spirit helps us in our weakness. We do not know what we ought to pray for, but the Spirit Himself intercedes for us through wordless groans. And He who searches our hearts knows the mind of the Spirit, because the Spirit intercedes for God's people in accordance with the will of God." Sometimes, you won't have the words to say, but the Holy Spirit will guide you. Sometimes, you will pray in tongues for hours, and then the Holy Spirit will guide you to a different route. If you don't have words to say, don't be afraid. To be honest, some of my best prayers came from desperation and not knowing what to say when in the middle of a struggle.

Watchman, arise like never before! Get on post! We are a team. The Holy Spirit gave me revelation about the body of Christ as a whole. In short, even though we don't know all of God's children by name, we are still working together and covering the nations as a team. There are so many people praying at certain times of the day, but we are still covering the world as one body. Ezekiel 3:17 states, "Son of man, I have made you a watchman for the people of Israel; so hear the word I speak and give them warning from me." It's so important to intercede and pray unto the Lord. Ephesians

6:18 states, "Praying always with all prayer and supplication in the Spirit and watching thereunto with all perseverance and supplication for all saints."

Stay on watch, warrior, and if you're feeling tired, find godly ways to get refueled because we all need you. It's important to take care of our bodies.

Below, you will find the different watch hours. Begin to track the time when you are most alert or whenever God awakens you. Be sure to purchase the watchman tracker so you can track your watch hours for a month. If you are not woken up frequently, and there is not a specific watch hour that you're assigned to, make sure you're recording the time you spend with God in prayer.

- **First Watch**—6:00pm-9:00pm
- **Second Watch**—9:00pm-12:00am
- **Third Watch**—12:00am-3:00am

- **Fourth Watch**—3:00am- 6:00am
- **Fifth Watch**—6:00am-9:00am
- **Sixth Watch**—9:00am-12:00am
- **Seventh Watch**—12:00am-3:00am
- **Eighth Watch**—3:00am-6:00pm

Warriors

We are all warriors, and that's why the Lord tells us to put on the whole armor of God. The breakdown of God's armor is not just published in the Bible, it is a literal charge to prepare yourself for war and stay covered. There are so many war movies that describe the importance of the intercessors in the body of Christ. We must make sure our sword is sharp and is being used daily. Don't get familiar with the weapons of the spirit that you have.

Oftentimes, in war movies, we see the concept of no man left behind. There will be some soldiers who will risk it all and rush to rescue someone who is in the line of fire. This life we have is no joke. We are all going through situations and challenges. Did you know that there are some people who are walking through life with no armor on? Imagine watching a war movie and everybody had their gear on except one person. That individual has jeans and a tee-shirt on. He would be the first target of the enemy, wouldn't he? As children of

God and intercessors, we can no longer walk around naked while on this journey called life.

I can remember this vision like it was yesterday. I was shaking in my armor, and another soldier handed me my sword. It's so important to know who you are. Even though I was shaking in my armor, I was able to understand the importance of picking up my sword and using it against the enemy. As warriors, we must know the direction in which the enemy tries to come. The enemy tries to come against me with fear. Now that I'm able to identify how he likes to get me off track, I'm able to put up the sword of the Spirit and slice his demonic devices and plans in half. The enemy is scared of you. The enemy knows that every knee must bow and every tongue must confess that Jesus Christ is Lord, according to Philippians 2:10. Jesus Himself went to hell and took the keys from the enemy. When you're facing anything, please know that you are an heir of Jesus Christ, and you have already won. Warrior, arise like never before! Intercessors are like the warriors who hide out in the bushes. We are called to be disguised at times. In those times, we are camouflaged or hidden so that we can get access to information. Once we get access to that information, we create prayer points to address. We are atomic bombs in the spirit realm for our families, churches, nations and world. At anytime, God should be able to drop us out of His airplane carrying the burden needed for the territory He has called us to. We must be on call 24/7.

While growing up, I remember always staying ready to minister to God's people and strangers through intercession. At family functions, I loved the times that we prayed together and for one another. Always remember the same power that rose Jesus from the dead lives inside of you. When you receive a prayer point, you are the vessel God is using to intercede. If God gives you a prayer point, imagine yourself in your armor being transported to that territory and being dropped there to cause confusion in the enemy's camp. Many of the times when the warriors are dropped out of the airplanes, they go in groups. We work together as intercessors. Just like the SWAT goes out in groups, there are times when God allows us to work as teams. When you have a group of intercessors at all borders, we are able to annihilate the enemy on a greater level. All the same, the prayer point God gives you shows the importance of being sensitive to the Spirit of the Lord. Get low, warrior. If you have to, lie on the floor. It gets rough sometimes. God will give you the strength that you need. Protecting God's people is an honor and privilege. If you notice that your brother or sister is struggling, imagine carrying them on your back. As you pray for others, God will strengthen you. Of course, we aren't superheroes, but the Holy Spirit will guide you, even if you have to refer a person to another intercessor other than yourself. There were many times when I needed prayer, but God dropped an assignment on me to intercede for someone else. Every time this happened, He took care of me and those I was carrying.

Chapter 5

The Throne Room

Every person reading this book is an intercessor. We each have access to the throne room as well. Jesus wants to see and hear from you more in the throne room. Jesus is our greatest example of an intercessor. He was on the cross interceding for us while He was lifted high. In Luke 23:34, Jesus said, "Father, forgive them, for they do not know what they are doing." We each have the right and access to the throne room. I'm believing that God will take you to His throne room in visions, dreams and trances. As intercessors, the throne room is our favorite place because we meet God there to have our discussions. We can enter into His throne room at any time or place. It's not about the earthly location. We receive directions, codes, secrets and even more. The throne room is a sacred place, and it is the best invitation you could ever receive. As intercessors, the throne room is where we go to God concerning His people and where we receive our instructions. Hebrews 4:16 states, "Let us then with confidence draw near to the throne of grace, that we may receive mercy and find grace to help in time of need." You are worthy. Don't allow thoughts or anything to strip you away from your inheritance. We are children of God. Since we are His children, we carry His DNA. We also get the benefits because we belong to Him. I challenge you in your prayer time today to go to the throne room boldly.

Decree and declare things over your life and those around you. Speak life over your family, church, nation, enemies and coworkers. The throne room is an intimate place, and it should be made a normal dwelling place for the intercessor. I remember it like it was yesterday. I experienced one of my first trances in the throne room. It was like being in two places at once. I had on an all-white garment, and I had a body posture of surrender right at the throne room of God. It was a beautiful place. The figure I was standing before was beyond huge, and I was so tiny. I could not see the face because the figure was so high. The place was so beautiful; it looked nothing like Earth. It was like being in a separate atmosphere besides Earth. I truly believe it was Heaven.

There have been many times the Lord has taken me to the heavens, but this time was very different. This happened right after I repented and went through deliverance in a way I had never received deliverance before. I confessed to the Lord that I needed help and even deliverance from trying to control His hand. I also needed deliverance from fear. Shortly after this, He took me to the throne time and time again. Don't be embarrassed or think you have to hide from the Lord. He knows everything and He wants you to come to Him.

Be free and let the Father hold your hand like never before. If anything is holding you back that nobody knows about, be free in this moment, in Jesus' name! He loves you and wants to hold you even closer and tighter.

Chapter 6

Marching Orders

Intercessors, it's time to arise like never before and stay on post. God is calling us to another level of intercession as the body of Christ. There are many ways we are able to focus. First, we must make sure we are warriors in the spirit and our weapons are being sharpened. We must renew our yes to the Lord. Intercession is not something everyone runs to, but it's one of the best ministries that we could ever submit to. Jesus Christ interceded for us while He was on the cross. Luke 23:34 states, "Then Jesus said, 'Father, forgive them, for they do not know what they do.'" Intercession requires sacrifice. Jesus was interceding while He was on the cross for each and every person. The call of intercession is so important. We must stick together as warriors, advocates, CIA Agents and watchmen. At different times, we will be different types of agents. As intercessors, God may wake you up in the middle of the night to pray for a country or even our prospective churches. Make sure you cover the prayer points God gives you. Intercede with humility and love. Never pray to get things, but pray because God has called you to intercede for the nations.

Fasting is very important. Many times when I'm fasting, God reveals sensitive information to me, including numbers and codes. Make sure you're staying before the Lord and fasting. When you fast, make sure you have a journal and write down anything that He shows you. I like to write in my journal while fasting, and after that, I have to debrief. It's important to fast weekly. God will put people and different prayer points in your heart to fast for. Fasting is very powerful. As a young child, I would fast for different people and would see breakthroughs. And you don't have to tell anyone. Be humble while fasting. In Matthew 6:16, it states, "Moreover when ye fast, be not, as the hypocrites, of sad countenance: for they disfigure their faces, that they may appear unto men to fast. Verily I say unto you, they have their reward. But when you fast, put your head and wash your face." I have had to repent because I told a person that I was fasting, but not intentionally. It's so intimate and should be kept between you and the Lord. Find books on fasting, and make sure you're still staying healthy as well. God doesn't want you to be sick. If fasting from food is a struggle for you, find other things you can fast from and, of course, be sure to seek guidance from a doctor or professional.

We must be in His Word daily, otherwise, our armor will become rusty. We will be intercessors who know how to use the power God has given us. We will not shoot out the blank ammunition of opinions and false doctrine, but we will release God's Word against the enemy.

I have gone through several deliverance sessions these past years, and each one has been amazing. I had one of the greatest encounters when I surrendered to the Lord. Warriors, when you decide to address every spirit and stronghold that tried to hold you and your bloodline back, your armor will become sharper. I knew there was another time of deliverance coming for me. Every time God wants to do something in me, He gives me a warning in some type of way. I remember being on a bench in a garden, and I was sitting on my brother's lap frozen and mute. That's when the Lord brought me to a back room where there was a beautiful beach right outside. I wouldn't move as I lay my head on my brother. There was a familiar spirit on one of my parents' side of the family that tried to attack the females in our bloodline. This spirit tried to destroy the prophetic assignment on some of the women. This spirit tried to attack and silence me in this vision. It wanted to destroy the prophetic assignment on my life. It was a spirit of depression, witchcraft and oppression. That devil tried to destroy our minds. At times, it would cause us to be mute. Not many weeks later, God ended up taking me through another deliverance; this broke chains off me that went back several generations. I was free because I surrendered. My whole bloodline is free. I'm so thankful for every deliverance and every person God has used and will use to walk me through deliverance. Shortly after I stood up, a horn went off. It may have been a coincidence, but I truly believe it was God bringing significance to that moment. God has the power to go all the way back and dismantle any spirit that would even think to try and destroy His people. We have the rights to and benefits of freedom. If you notice a generational curse in your bloodline, address it and get healed. When I received this particular deliverance, I manifested very strongly. I was leaning back at angles I can't explain. I was coughing up a lot as well and crying. I was leaning back like the character in the Matrix movie, but I walked out as free as a bird.

Put your armor on. We need to be warriors who are steps ahead of the devices of the enemy. Don't ever get comfortable and start thinking you will not need it. We must keep our armor on at all times. If your armor has not been on, I challenge you to get the training you need. There are so many ways that you can train. Start a daily prayer schedule and stick to it. Get involved in a prayer group. Be in your Word daily. There are so many apps and Bible classes that you can find. Ask the Holy Spirit to guide you to what you should listen to. You can even go on YouTube. I endured years of turmoil in my mind because I did not use the weapons God has given me. God has given us the Holy Spirit and His Word to guide us through any situation we face. Do not grieve the Holy Spirit, but yield to how He leads you. It's a matter of knowing what areas you need to train in. In the vision where I saw myself shaking in my armor, another soldier gave me my sword. This vision also made me more aware of the areas I needed to train my spiritual muscles in. If you allow the Holy Spirit to train you, He will do it. Stay focused, warrior, because you are a whole dynamite. I went from shaking in my gear to slaying the demons that tried to hold me down. I remember a vision of me using my sword and destroying about eight demons at once. We must train our spiritual muscles. If it helps, you can write down each part of the armor and see how you can incorporate responses in every area of your daily life. We need the shield of faith for every situation that we face. In life, not everything is going to go the way we've planned it; in fact, Jesus has a funny way of taking us on a roller coaster ride of faith. Have faith in God and know that He will take care of you. When the enemy tries to tell you lies through opinions or even self-doubt, let it roll off your back like water, and realize that you wear the belt of truth. Your belt of truth allows you to shoot down words that are contrary to God's Word. Tell the devil to SHUT UP and blow the Word of God on him so he can melt. Warrior, the Word of God is your defense. The helmet of salvation gives us the comfort and security we need, knowing that we are citizens of the Kingdom of God. Do you know that you are your heavenly Father's child? Bring your sword out, which again represents God's Word, and shred every lie into pieces. The Word helps us to have the right responses to every situation that we face. Consecration is important, as children of God and intercessors. There are so many ways that we can consecrate. There are times where we have to consecrate from food, people, places and even what we watch. Allow the Holy Spirit to lead you. Be careful what you watch. There have been so many times when the Holy Spirit told me not to go see a movie that everybody else was going to see. As intercessors, be sensitive to the spirit. As a child, I started to consecrate at a young age. I was not perfect at it all the time, of course. When I started consecrating at a young age, I heard the Holy Spirit at greater heights. Be careful of the television shows that you watch. The diet of the intercessor is important. If you're feeding your spirit movies filled with sex, profanity, terror, etc., you will begin to digest what you've consumed. Ask the Holy Spirit what are ways that He wants you to consecrate. The Holy Spirit speaks to me even concerning the music that I listen to. We want to protect our ear gates. We want to consecrate in everything we do to bring glory to God. There have been times when I dreamed about songs that I played that day. There may be CDs, magazines and other forms of media that you need to discard. There is nothing that God can't deliver His children from. If you find yourself having trouble giving up things, there are so many ways you can seek counsel. Seek counseling, deliverance or even mentorship. Don't consecrate once or twice a year, but try to incorporate it in your everyday life. God may tell you to go on 15-day social media fast. Be sensitive to the voice of God. There are so many examples of ways to consecrate, but everyone is different. Don't look at how God tells others to consecrate; we are all different. Just be led by the Holy Spirit.

If there is any way that you can bring back prayer to your job, I challenge you to do it, mighty warrior. I remember working at a company where they had a Bible study that met once a week. Talk to your human resources department and ask if there are ways to start a Bible study or even a prayer group. We need to make prayer normal again everywhere that we go. This Bible study helped me so much throughout the day. I even invited others to come. This is an opportunity to evangelize and lead souls to Christ. Any opportunity to spread the gospel of Jesus Christ is an honor. Some people may not come to church, but at least you dropped the seed in their spirit. If you're in school or even college, find out how you can start a prayer group. Some colleges have hundreds of different activities. A prayer group should also be a part of those activities. Can you imagine if there were prayer groups back in the schools all over the world? I remember when I was growing up and I was in grade school, there were so many activities to choose from, but there wasn't anything centered around prayer. Some schools have gospel choirs. If they allow choirs, surely they should allow prayer and Bible study groups. I grew so much having the different Bible study groups on campus. Prayer and Bible study groups help us stay accountable. Intercession at our jobs and schools could open up a door for the Chief Executive Officers and the deans to call on the intercessors when the schools or companies have unmet needs or when tragedy hits. We want to intercede everywhere we go and in all that we do. Can you imagine the dean of a college calling you to pray over the new freshmen coming in? I will take it to another level. It should be to the point where the Dean calls forth intercessors to pray over the campus for three days before the new students come onto the campus. I remember being a little girl, and my school had us take prayer requests. After this, they scheduled us to make house visits to pray for those we received prayer requests from.

It's very important for churches to also have prayer groups. If your church does not have a prayer group, go through your chain of command and find out ways that you could start one. The churches need intercessors of all ages. Every church should have some type of prayer group. Praying together as the body of Christ all on one accord changes things. Acts 2 states, "When the day of Pentecost came, they were all together in one place." Imagine two soldiers, but then imagine 5,000 intercessors praying. If we, as intercessors, were to all come together on one accord, lifting our voices and covering the nations, we would definitely make a change. We must make intercession normal all over the nation. Ecclesiastes 4:9-12 states, "Two are better than one, because they have good return for their labor: If either of them falls down, one can help the other up." As intercessors, we carry and hold each other up.

Die to Self

We must die to self in so many areas of our lives. As intercessors, we can't just pray for the things we want to pray for. We must be able to pray for everyone else, including our enemies. Never speak evil of anybody that you are put under. Pray for the political leaders, your boss and your supervisors, etc. If you find someone speaking evil about any political leader, shut it down and say, "Let's pray that God leads them." If you find yourself not being able to pray for someone because you are offended by that person, pray and ask the Lord for guidance, and speak with that person. We do not want to leave any room for the enemy.

Matthew 5: 23 states, "Therefore if thou bring thy gift to the altar, and there remembers that thy brother hath ought against thee; leave there thy gift before the altar, and go thy way; first be reconciled to thy brother, and then come and offer thy gift." There have been times when I have had to repent for not handling situations correctly. It's important to ask the Holy Spirit to scan your heart. We are all learning and growing. As intercessors, we are called to pray for everyone. Matthew 5:44 states, "But I say unto you. Love your enemies, bless them that curse you, do good to them that hate you, pray for them that which despitefully use you, and persecute you." Warrior, train your mind to pray for everyone. As an intercessor, you must completely die to yourself. Jesus died for everyone. He did not just die for the people who believed, but for the ones who did not believe. He died for the ones who mocked and beat Him. Jesus is our greatest example of an intercessor. While on the cross, He asked God to forgive those who were crucifying Him. He was very selfless and humble. Always remain humble in every area of your life. To truly be like Jesus, we must love like Him. It's not easy, but if you spend time with Him and let Him work on your heart, you will stop cussing people out in traffic. We should be to the point where we are no longer speaking curses over people, but we should be asking the Holy Spirit to teach us how to respond. We truly serve a God who loves us. One of the many scriptures that have changed my life is 2 Chronicles 7:14, which reads, "If my people, which are called by name, shall humble themselves, and pray and seek my face, and turn from their wicked ways; then I will hear from heaven, and will forgive their sin and will heal their land." Warriors, when you sit and dissect this verse, you gain so much revelation each time. I remember when the Holy Spirit called me to a consecration concerning this scripture. My life changed. He began to show me things about myself that needed to be destroyed in me. The Lord revealed to me that I must be my own intercessor first, and I must be ready to receive the correction and rebuke from the Holy Spirit. The Holy Spirit has rebuked me in love many times, but I have grown each time. I told God during this time of consecration that I'm turning away from every evil thing that is not pleasing to Him. God speaks to His children differently. Seek the Lord for your guidance.

To be honest with you, there was a part of me that really needed to die. I loved to twerk. I mean in competitions, and even on top of tables and chairs. Don't get me wrong, twerking is not bad when you're married, and that's why God said I needed to save it for my husband. You'd better believe my twerks will be revived when that day comes. I made twerking an idol that needed to be destroyed. I had to delete certain songs that I would play over and over again. If you ask the Lord, He will show you what you need to consecrate from. I began to love twerking more than God. To be honest, it started to be an addiction. He allowed me to understand that it's not bad to twerk, but for me, it's just the importance of knowing where I should do it and with whom. Romans 14:16 states, "Let not then your good be evil spoken of." God was taking me through a stripping, and it has been the best process I have been through. The more I got naked, the closer I got to Him. The more I dealt with self, the freer I became.

Growing up, my parents raised me and my brother by the instruction of the Holy Spirit. My mom would always sit me down and remind me of the importance of repenting from my iniquities. She would always tell me the importance of knowing the many ways the enemy would try and cause me to fall into sin, and how to address it. Ephesians 4:29 states, "Let no corrupting talk come out of your mouths, but only such as is good for building up, as fits the occasion, that it may give grace to those who hear." My parents also taught my brother and I the importance of never using your mouth to harm others in any shape or form. I never heard my parents gossip or belittle anyone. I remember growing up and hearing people say, "Be careful what you say around her (referring to my mother) because God could show her the conversations we shouldn't be having." People should be uncomfortable around you bringing down others.

Prayer:

◆ Lord, today, I decide to crucify my flesh like I never have. I repent for selfish intentions and motives. Lord, help me to be more like You in my actions and in all that I do. In Galatians 5:24, it states, "And those who belong to Christ Jesus have crucified the flesh with its passions and desires." Let there be no area in my life where You are absent. I welcome You in every area of my life. Cleanse my heart and mind. Lord, I repent for any

idols in my life. Lord, I draw closer to
You on this day. I renew my yes to You,
in Jesus' name. Amen.

Chapter 7

Undefeated

Do you know that you are already undefeated regardless of what you may be facing? Jesus Christ died on the cross and took all power from the enemy before saving us. Where in the Bible can we look and find it saying that Jesus is defeated? NOWHERE!! We serve a God who is all powerful and has given us dominion power as well. There are no tests or trials that you can't make it through. Whenever you face a challenge, be so deep in your Word that your spirit will automatically quote Isaiah 54:17, "No weapon formed against us shall prosper." Anytime you feel defeated, remember you are a child of God and you are His mighty intercessor. God can use us all at different times in the form of a warrior, CIA agent, watchman or even an advocate. At times, we are all of them at once, depending on what we are facing. Imagine the first day of training for the army, and in the first meeting, the sergeant states that the enemy is already defeated. Since we serve a God that has already defeated the enemy, every situation and challenge, we can already decree that we are undefeated. We can also ask the Lord for wisdom and strength to walk through this thing called life. Since we are heirs of Jesus Christ and He took the keys from hell with all power and might, we are victorious. Luke 10:19 states, "Behold, I give unto you power to tread on serpents and scorpions, and all the power of the enemy; and nothing shall by any means hurt you." Soldier, read this scripture every day and memorize it. We serve a God who has already given us victory over our enemies. Jeremiah 51:20 states, "Thou art my battle ax and weapons of war for with thee will I break in pieces the nations, and with thee will I destroy kingdoms." Congratulations, you have already won! There was a time when I dealt with fear so badly that I didn't like speaking up. My mom said, "Man can't do anything to you." I asked, "What if they destroy me?" And she said, "He will resurrect you." When you are a child of God, you can't lose, regardless of the situation.

Intercessors are emotional and sensitive, and because we are sensitive, we have to allow the Holy Spirit to direct us. Have you ever experienced great joy, but then you go somewhere and start to feel depressed? There was a time when I did not fully understand this phenomena, as an intercessor. I used to be left in a ditch of depression and anxiety, and what I was experiencing weren't my own emotions. Once I began to learn that every emotion I feel is not my own, I began praying in the moments when I experienced negative emotions. If I'm around people and I feel a heavy burden to pray, I will ask the person if I can pray for him or her, and we will pray wherever we are. Allow the Holy Spirit to lead you. You are very powerful because your heavenly Father is omnipotent (all-powerful). The Word states in Acts 5:15, "As a result, people brought the sick into the streets and laid them on beds and mats so that at least Peter's shadow might fall on some of them as he passed by." Your presence alone makes the enemy nervous. You don't even have to speak, and the enemy knows that just by your presence, he has to flee. Arise, intercessor! Arise! I started dealing with extreme sensitivity between the ages of three and six. I would carry so much, and I needed to learn the importance of lifting those prayers up to the Lord. When I learned that every emotion wasn't my own, my joy was increased. Intercessors, open up your mouths and rebuke the enemy. Anytime he tries to appear big, remember that he is under your feet. My mom would tell me when I was little that he is a little dog with a loud bark. Kick the enemy out! Kick him off your home, thoughts, emotions, families, job, etc. He is the father of lies! No fear. God is ahead, behind and all around you!

Do you know the power that you hold? Let me remind you of the power of your prayers. In Acts 16:25, it states, "About midnight Paul and Silas were praying and singing hymns to God, and the other prisoners were listening to them. Suddenly there was such a violent earthquake that the foundations of the prison were shaken. At once all the prison doors flew open, and everyone's chains came loose." Even throughout the tests and trials, it may feel like there is no way out. I dare you to stand up wherever you are and begin to praise Him. Your prayers and praises have the power to turn things around. Paul and Silas had to recognize the power that they had throughout their hard situations. No demon, witch, or warlock can stop the hand of God. You have the power within you to decree God's Word and cause the enemy to be destroyed. God is powerful, intercessor. But of course, make sure you are living holy and staying pure before the

Lord. If you ever find yourself not having peace, John 16:33 states, "I have said these things to you, that in my you may have peace. In the world, you will have tribulation. But take heart; I have overcame the world." We have a right to peace, no matter what we go through. God knew we would go through hard times, so He already gave us our inheritance of peace. This explains why, in the most challenging times of my life, I had peace. Have you ever gone through something and had people ask you why you were so happy? It's the peace of God, and we can have it no matter what!! Don't give up and don't quit!! You are powerful! You're going to get through this!!

The Battle is Not Yours

We serve an incredible God! What kind of God can tell you that you have already won the battle? Our God is the GREAT I AM! He has already defeated the enemy. All we have to do is declare the truth of what has already been decreed and completed. You are very powerful because the Spirit of Lord lives within you! 2 Chronicles 20:15 states, "He said; 'Listen, King Jehoshaphat and all who live in Judah and Jerusalem! This is what the Lord says to you; 'Do not be afraid or discouraged because of this vast army. For the battle is not yours, but God's.'" Through the Word of God, we are able to see that God has already fought the battles for us, and no weapon formed against shall prosper. The Lord is our Chief and General. To hear that the battle has already been won and no opponent can destroy us is comforting. If God allows us to know that the battle is not ours because it belongs to the Lord, what does that mean for us? We are undefeated. No matter what you go through or what you face, believe that God already has everything under control and in His hands. In life, we face real life situations, but we must sharpen our armor. Since His Word is true, He is going to get the glory, even through the hard things. There have been so many times that I threw off my armor and thought I couldn't face another day by myself. Keep your head up, even through those times when you want to quit. God is right there beside you, and He will lift your head. Psalms 3:3 states, "But you, Lord, are a shield around me, my glory, the One who lifts my head high." There are times that we will cry, scream and ask God why we're going through whatever it is that we're going through, but we must hold on because we don't serve a God who will ever leave or forsake us. There will be seasons we ask, "God, where are You?" When this happens, let your shield of faith be held high, and be reminded that He is going to make a way. To be honest, there are times when we want to throw our shield of faith on the ground and walk away. But if we push through and hold that shield of faith high, He will see us through. Since the battle is not ours, but the Lord's, we still have to wear our armor and make sure that it stays sharp and crisp. There will be times when we are on the ground, and we feel like we are crawling, but be of good courage.

Warriors need encouragement, especially if they have been carrying others. Isaiah 40:28 states, "Do you not know? Have you not heard? The Everlasting God, the Lord, the Creator of the ends of the earth does not become weary or tired. His understanding is inscrutable. He gives strength to the weary, and to Him who lacks might He increases power." As warriors, we have to admit when we are tired and ask the Lord for the strength that we need. Speak to the Lord, and tell Him what you need. He is our friend and our comforter. Don't ever be afraid to come to your heavenly Father and tell Him how you feel. God wants us to be transparent with Him. Even though I know God knows everything about me, the fact that I can come to Him in tears or smiles, and tell Him how I feel, helps me to grow so much closer to Him.

Chapter 8

Holy Spirit

Being best friends with the Holy Spirit has been
the best decision I have ever made since I was
a child. I knew of the Holy Spirit at a young
age. I felt Him so strongly and heard His voice,
even as a little girl. It's so important to have an
intimate relationship with the Lord and receive
the gift of the Holy Spirit. The Holy Spirit is a
GPS who guides God's people, especially
intercessors. Intercessors must lean on the
Holy Spirit because He gives us instructions
and shows us the direction in which we are to
go. Sometimes, you will have so many prayer
points that you need to seek the Lord for, and
you have to ask the Holy Spirit to lead and
guide you. The Holy Spirit is not only a GPS,
but a friend. The Holy Spirit will come in the
room at any time and bring comfort to your

heart. The Holy Spirit is a gift who came after Jesus Christ went up to be with God. The Holy Spirit will convict, correct, direct and lead you as a Teacher. The Holy Spirit will teach you how to treat people, and give you the right heart and spirit. Make sure you call the Holy Spirit's name out and say, "Holy Spirit, lead and guide me." Spend time with the Holy Spirit. Invite the Holy Spirit in every area of your life. Make sure you have conversations that the Holy Spirit can sit and listen to. But wait a minute, He listens to all of our conversations anyway. This is why He is all-knowing. Make sure you're always creating an atmosphere where Jesus Christ can have a seat. The Holy Spirit loves when you speak with Him. The Holy Spirit will guide you in all things. John 14:26 states, "But the Helper, the Holy Spirit, whom the Father will send in my name,He will teach you all things and bring to your remembrance all that I have said to you." Always remember that whenever God uses you, what comes out of you did not come from you, it came through you. We are only vessels. We not only have the Holy Spirit, but God allows heavenly ministering angels to watch over us. Luke 4:10 states, "For it is written, 'He will command His angels concerning you, to guard you.'" I started seeing angels when I was in my early teens. Over the years, I have seen different forms of angels. Sometimes, I will see their wings (they are pure white), or I will see them standing watch at my window. I remember one time, I noticed one of my angels, and the Lord told me to command my angel to go on an assignment. Sometimes, they appear in physical form, or I will see them in dreams or visions. I mainly see them in physical form. I have seen them in all sizes. Some of them have been as big as commercial buildings. Each of us has angels. Activate your angels. Do you know your angels can even minister to you? 1 Kings 19:7 states, "And the angel of the Lord came again the second time, and touched him, and said, Arise and eat; because the journey is too great for thee." We do not worship angels. Angels are ministers and vessels who God uses. There have been many times when angels have touched me and even yanked me out of my bed to pray. There was a time when I felt a heavenly touch; it lifted me out of my bed and alerted me to pray for a person. I also remember a time when I felt so heavy and an angel wrapped his wings around me. I decree that the angels of Heaven assigned to you will activate like never before. Angels protect and even bring messages. I have had instances where angels led me to leave a place. Angels will minister to you as you minister to others. There are times when you pray for others, but you're tired and God will strengthen you. I have had many encounters when I was weak, but God strengthened me and the angels were surrounding me. When you're praying for souls to be saved, angels can assist you by going and ministering to that person.

There was a time when I sent my angels to

allow my name to go into rooms that I needed for favor. I had one of the hardest professors in college, and I did not complete my paper. This paper was supposed to be about sixty pages in length, and I only completed about thirty pages. This was the final paper. I knew I was going to fail this class, but then I prayed in that dorm room for the Lord to soften his heart and allow the angels to minister to him. He ended up writing me the nicest comment, and gave me a high score. Our prayers and words have power. Stay encouraged. God has given us access and assistance, even when we are tired.

There are so many types of angels in the Bible. I'm going to discuss just a few. There are the cherubim angels found in Ezekiel 1. Ezekiel 1:5 states, "Also out of the midst thereof came the likeness of four living creatures. And this was their appearance; they had the likeness of a man. And every one had four faces, and everyone had four wings. And their feet was straight feet; and the sole of their feet was like the sole of a calf's foot; and they sparkled like the color of burnished brass." Ezekiel 10:5 states, "And the sound of the cherubim's wings was heard even to the outer court, as the voice of the Almighty God when He speaketh." We also find in Isaiah 6 the description of Seraphim angels. Satan, Michael and Gabriel are also angels discussed in the Bible. There are angels of Heaven, and there are fallen angels. Satan is considered a fallen angel. Michael is mentioned in Jude 1:9. Some of these angels are mentioned throughout the Bible. Gabriel was also the angel God sent to tell Mary about the birth of Jesus in Luke 1. Don't be afraid of the supernatural. The Bible gives us so much information on angels. Begin to read scriptures about angels so you can gain more knowledge. Don't be afraid; we all have angels assigned to us! Activate the angels God assigned to you TODAY!!

It's very important to treat people with love. Hebrews 13:2 states, "Be not forgetful to entertain strangers for thereby some have entertained angels unawares." You never know who you are amongst. It's important not to make fun of anybody or make people feel bad about themselves. It doesn't matter if they can hear you or not, because the One who matters can hear you.

Supernatural Intercession

During my life, I have experienced supernatural intercession in many different ways from our Savior, Jesus Christ. Earlier in this book, I mentioned the time my feet scooted into someone's home while I was praying with my mother. It felt like I was on top of water. God gave me a preview of their issues so that I could pray and cover their home. Supernatural intercession allows you to experience Heaven on Earth while interceding to God, our Father. According to Merriam Webster, the supernatural is defined as: "of or relating to an order of existence beyond the visible observable universe". The supernatural can be in the way of dreams, trances, visions, angels, glory dust, smoke or even feathers falling from Heaven. There is no limit to how God wants us to encounter Him. Many people in the Bible experienced the supernatural or even witnessed it. Elisha witnessed the supernatural. 2 Kings 2:11-12 states, "As they were walking along and talking together, suddenly a chariot of fire and horse of fire appeared and separated the two of them, and Elijah went up to heaven in a whirlwind. Elisha saw this and cried out, 'My father! My father! The chariots and horsemen of Israel!' And Elisha saw him no more. Then he took hold of his garment and tore it into two." Supernatural intercession allows you to experience Heaven while interceding. Matthew 13:11 states, "He replied, Because the knowledge of the secrets of the kingdom of heaven has been given to you, but not to them." Ask the Lord to open your heart. Ask our Savior, Jesus Christ, to show you the mysteries of Heaven and His Kingdom. There was a time when I asked God to show me the mysteries of the Kingdom of Heaven, and that same night I had an encounter with God. He lifted me out of my bed and the room froze. I heard His voice loud and clear saying, "Oh ye of little faith," during a time I was lacking faith. This encounter encouraged me to never doubt God or put limits on what He can do.

Wash the Feet of God's People
It's essential to always know that you are a servant of the Lord. Looking over my life, I have experienced more joy than I have ever had serving the Lord. Make sure whatever God has called you to do, you do it unto the Lord. Make sure you serve with gladness and a joyful heart. Whenever I have an assignment for the Lord, I get beyond excited. Serving God's people is one of the best things you could ever do because that's what Christ did. John 13:4-5 states, "So He got up from the meal, took off His outer clothing and wrapped a towel around His waist. After that, He poured

water into a basin and began to wash His disciples feet, drying them with the towel that was wrapped around Him." Jesus is the first example of everything He is calling us to be. He not only tells us to forgive and serve our brothers and sisters, but He demonstrated what this looked like. In other words, He led by example. Jesus washed the feet of everyone. He even washed Judas and Peter's feet. We must push past how we feel and really love the way Jesus has called us to love. It's not easy, but with the help of the Holy Spirit and having a loving and forgiving heart, we can do this as well. In everything you do, wash the feet of God's people. Always remember this paragraph when you want to give up on people. Colossians 3:23-24 states, "Whatever you do, work at it with all your heart, as working for the Lord, not for human masters, since you know that you will receive an inheritance from the Lord as a reward, it is the Lord Christ you are serving." These instructions are not limited to one thing, but they encompass everything we do in life. So, even on our jobs, schools, churches, etc., we must do this unto the Lord. I always think back to when I was working, and one of my coworkers said, "If you give Sarah the job of counting jelly beans, she would be happy." The Holy Spirit will lead and guide you on how to navigate through the difficulties of serving people, especially in the areas where it's hard for you. When God gives you a prayer point or a person to pray for, you're literally washing that person's feet. One of the many qualities that stands out to me about our God is His heart to serve. Jesus washed the feet of those He knew, even though He knew that one of them would betray Him. If some of us were put in Jesus Christ's shoes, we would have said, "I'm not washing your feet; you're going to betray me." Serving in God's Kingdom is the best thing you could ever do. Serving in my Father's house gives me a joy I can't explain. Serve without expecting. Serve out of love. Serve, not because you want to be seen, but serve

because that's the character our Father has.
Serve because that's how our Father showed
love to us without expecting anything in return.

Divorce

There came a time when I literally felt God
tearing me down to build me all the way back
up. I didn't feel like myself. It was like I was
transforming into a new person for His glory.
He then began to give me more interpretation
regarding what He was doing inside of me.
Intercessors, allow God to truly work on your
heart and mind. He told me that He no longer
wants to date me, but to marry me. The whole
time I thought I was married to Him, but He
said, "You ain't seen nothing yet." Once I said
yes to the process, I went through so many
deliverances. He kept stripping me over and
over again. Once I thought He was done, He
dipped me all over again. As He went layer by
layer, I felt like I was beginning to know Him
more than I have ever known Him. When God
told me that He wanted to marry me, He also

said I must divorce everything that has ever
tried to come against my relationship with Him.
During my walk, I faced every demon possible
that tried to stop me from getting my
deliverance. My identity was under so much
pressure because I did not know who I was.
God told me to divorce low self-esteem,
insecurity, fear, identity crisis and self-hate. It
was like the King was calling me. The King
truly wants to be married to you. He no longer
wants to date you. He wants to immerse you in
His love. Isaiah 62:5 states, "For as young man
marrieth a virgin, so shall thy sons marry thee:
and as the bridegroom rejoiceth over the bride,
so shall thy God rejoice over thee." God loves
you so much. God wants to love us all over
again with a new type of love each day. He
wants to love every part of us. Don't hold
anything back from your Lord. He is waiting
and ready to walk with you in every single area
of your life. I had to address every unclean
spirit and die to myself. In order for me to be
fully married to God, there were still areas in

my life I needed to invite Him into. Make sure you're inviting Him in all areas of your life. There is nothing that is too much for our God to handle. God literally created me all over again, and it's something I will never forget. I remember having a vision of a potter with his hands on clay. God confirmed that He was making me all over again. Don't be afraid of the process. The beautiful thing about it is the fact that it was His hands touching me. Being in the hands of God is the greatest comfort I have ever encountered. It's very important to stay committed to our heavenly Father. Once I decided to pursue God and give Him my all, things changed for me. It's like I no longer pursued earthly things, but Jesus Christ. Go after Him and pursue Him like never before. I have never felt so whole in my life!! Renew your vows to Him if you have to. Recommitting is something I truly had to do.

Prayer:

- ◆ Thank You, Lord, for this day. Today, I

lay everything at the cross. Lord, let there be no area in my life that You have not touched. I repent for any ways I have that are not pleasing to You. I denounce every spirit that is not of God. I divorce every way of wickedness and receive Your forgiveness and love. Lord, dip me in Your love all over again and show me the way. Walk with me, Lord. Hold me, Lord. Guide me in the areas that I need to get more counsel in. I no longer want to date You, but marry You. Fill me up with Your Holy Spirit, and make me new. Wash me, Lord. Transform me. Today, I recommit my life to You. I no longer want to date You, but marry You. In Jesus name. Amen.

Chapter 9

Charge to the Intercessor

Warriors, I charge you this day to recruit as many intercessors as possible. If you have an opportunity to pray for someone or witness to someone, DO IT! I'd gone out to eat one day, and there was a waitress taking care of me, and while she was serving me, the Lord revealed that her son was in the hospital. I thanked her for serving me, and I felt the presence of the Lord over her. I then spoke a blessing over her and brought up the topic of her son. She then confirmed that he was in the hospital. Let us be about our Father's business. Luke 2:49 states, "And He said to them, 'Why did you seek Me? Did you not know that I must be about My Father's business?" It's time to be about our Father's business like never before. Make sure you are focused on doing the will of the Father. Matthew 6:33 reads, "But seek ye first the kingdom of God, and His righteousness; and all these things shall be added unto you." Ask the Lord to give you the desire to do His business, and to mirror the works of the Father. As you lead souls to Christ, don't forget to remind them about the importance of intercession and having intimate time with the Lord, Jesus Christ. It would be awesome if you would even write down a few action steps to take right now. Ask the Lord to lead and guide you. Ask Him to open up your eyes and ears to see what you should be doing as you seek Him.

Good Fruit

Warriors, we must bear good fruit. It doesn't matter if you can call angels down from Heaven. John 15:16, "You did not choose me, but I chose you and appointed you that you should go and bear fruit and that your fruit should abide, so that whatever you ask the Father in my name, He may give it to you." We must bear good fruit. In order to bear good fruit, we must know the fruits of the Spirit. In Galatians 5:22 says, "But the fruit of the Spirit is love, joy, peace, longsuffering, gentleness, goodness, faith, meekness, temperance: against such there is no law. And they that are Christ's have crucified the flesh with the affections and lust. If we live in the Spirit let us also walk in the Spirit." We should do self-evaluations, especially on our fruit trees. Ever since I was a little girl, my mom has taught me the importance of self-evaluations. 1 Corinthians 13:1-4 states, "Though I speak with tongues of men and of angels, and have not love, I am become as sounding brass, or tinkling cymbal. And though I have the gift of prophecy and understand all mysteries, and all knowledge; and though I have all faith, so that I could remove mountains. and have not love, I am nothing. And though I bestow all my goods to feed the poor, and though I give my body to be burned and have not love, it profiteh me nothing. Love suffereth long, and is kind; love envieth not; love vaunteth not itself, is not puffed up." Let's make sure we are spreading love every chance we get. Our riches are in Heaven, and not on Earth. LOVE. LOVE. LOVE. 2 Corinthians 4:18, states, "So we fix our eyes not on what is seen, but on what is unseen, since what is seen is temporary, but what is unseen is eternal." Let us not be intercessors who pray Heaven down, but can't do the greatest of these, which is LOVE! Let us not be intercessors who can call Michael down, but can't love people. For example, when I was a little girl, my dad would volunteer as a minister to go and help the elderly. Let us never be so into ourselves that we can't love our neighbors. Of course, allow the Holy Spirit to lead you. We are humans, but we should at least be able to point someone in the right direction if we can't help ourselves.

The Holy Spirit spoke to me and made sure that my fruit tree was looking good. There have been times when I slacked and had bitter fruit.

We are not supposed to have fruit with nasty worms. We shouldn't be producing fruit that is gold on the outside, but rotten on the inside. If you notice that you're lacking in any of these areas, take some time to consecrate and target that area in prayer and fasting. 1 Corinthians 13:1 states, "Though I speak with the tongues of men and of angels, but have not charity, I am become as sounding brass or a tinkling cymbal." As intercessors, it's important to know that we can call Heaven down with our prayers, but if we do not truly love from our hearts, we are nothing but a loud sound. Lord, help us to show love like You! Lord, help us to be like You!

We must make sure that we take on the characteristics of our heavenly Father. God wants us to be healthy and love ourselves and others. There was a time when the fruit I was producing was so unclean that I did not even recognize myself anymore. I noticed I was lacking self-control. I used to hate myself so much that I picked up a cutting addiction. I not only didn't like myself, but I was mad at who I was. Little did I know that God loved me for me. I not only had a cutting addiction, but I was mad at God. I wanted Him to work on my time clock. I wanted my mom healed from a generational curse that tried to destroy my grandmother, her and I. I have addressed that spirit and it's destroyed with no return in the bloodline by the power of Jesus Christ. Through the challenges and waiting we must trust God. Lord, help us. I noticed my fruit tree was not producing good fruit. I not only had a cutting addiction, but I tried to commit suicide by taking over one hundred pills. I threw a tantrum with God because I wanted to control how He moved. When we think of witchcraft, we always imagine someone flying on a broom, but it can be in our everyday actions. Little did I know this situation drew me so much closer to God than I have ever been before. I remember being in the ICU, and the doctors said I had too many drugs in my system to go home. I had to go to a rehabilitation center. I remember the ER doctor evaluating my skin and identifying my bloody arm from the top of my wrist to where my IV was. He also noticed the older cuts. I had knives hidden all over the house. When I tell you that God met me at the ER and the hospitals, it's the truth. Every nurse and doctor had been sent by God, even the rehabilitation center's pastor. I remember sitting in group therapy and praying for God to meet me in a new way. Moments later, the hospital's pastor asked to speak with me privately. He assigned a female mentor to me who I still have contact with to date. This happened about ten years ago. I felt the presence of the Lord all over that place. This was the place that God truly renewed my mind through counseling and therapy. God even gave me the opportunity to minister to those who were broken. There were people who had a long list of mental disorders, and some of them were even violent. When I walked into the therapy room, everyone stopped and looked at me. One woman stated,

"You don't look like us." Til this day, I wonder why she said that. She must have noticed something different about me. There was a person who did not even believe in God, but amazingly enough, he allowed me to read some scriptures to him. You can minister to people no matter where you're at in life. In my weakest moments, I would think that I wouldn't have the strength to speak, but God gave me the strength to minister. I remember staying up all night one time because we had an assignment to write down one hundred coping skills. I was in a room with a lady, and she confided in me, saying that she was in rehabilitation because she tried to commit suicide over 12 times. She told me she couldn't finish the one hundred-page assignment. I decided to not only finish my assignment, but to help her finish her assignment as well. There was a time when I threw all my armor off and gave up on God. I tried diligently to control the hand of God. I had to learn to truly trust in God, even in my thinking. The cutting was so bad I would go buy makeup to cover up the scars on top of the dry blood. God gave me revelation to no longer hide my scars because they are beautiful battle scars. I did not know how to deal with the spirit of rejection, self-hatred, low self-esteem, etc. I always felt like I was different and never fit in. God's Word says in 1 Peter 2:9 that we are peculiar people. I used to hate the distinctive characteristics I had that made me different, but now I love myself the way God does. Do you know we all have one fingerprint in Christ? What makes us different makes each of us special. Your difference can bless a whole nation and produce masterpieces. God wants us healthy mentally, physically and spiritually. Take time out to make sure you're healthy in each area. Once I decided to face everything, I became stronger on the battlefield. Counseling and therapy are very important for the intercessor because we see and sense so much. We are very sensitive, and it's not a bad thing at all to be sensitive. It's just how the gift works.

Counseling was the best thing I could ever decide to get. I can't emphasize on this enough. Proverbs 11:14 states, "Where no counsel is, the people fall: but in the multitude of counsellors there is safety."Counseling, mentorship, deliverance and therapy are so important; they helped me so much. Don't be afraid of any of them. If I hadn't went through any of these, I would not be who I am today. I was always the child who liked to be around adults. I loved to receive the wisdom they shared. My mom and dad have been my best friends since I was a little girl. They trained and raised me by the leading of the Holy Spirit. They helped me to understand the call upon my life. My grandpa also helped me through college. He would keep me on the phone for hours for Bible study. He discipled me in the Lord. I'm so thankful for his leadership. His teachings still help me. He taught me the importance of staying on my knees in prayer and feeding on the Word of God daily. Rejection was a stronghold over my life, and it needed to be broken. I idolized people's words over God's Word. It's very important to make sure people's opinions don't speak louder than your purpose and assignment. You have an assignment to destroy the works of the enemy. What if Jesus did not complete His assignment because He cared more about what people said or didn't say than His own assignment? If Jesus acted on rejection like we do, we wouldn't be where we are right now. The Lord could have run away lamenting about people not liking Him, but He didn't. If you do not know your purpose, spend time with the Father and let Him minister to you. Every person born has an assignment to usher in God's glory. Intercessor, do not allow the spirit of rejection to tie you down from being all that God has called you to be. Rejection is demonic. It is not a part of the Kingdom of God. In fact, Romans 14:17 says, "For the kingdom of God is not meat and drink; but righteousness, and peace, and joy in the Holy Ghost." Don't eat from any other kingdom's table; only eat from the table of your heavenly Father. Can you imagine Jesus feeding into the emotional side of rejection? If Jesus waited until the Pharisees accepted Him, He would still be waiting. There are still people who do not believe that Jesus Christ is the Messiah. We each have a purpose and assignment in the body of Christ. 1 Corinthians 12:12, "Just as a body, though one, has many parts, but all its many parts form one body, so it is with Christ." Everyone reading this book has an assignment. We all have been made uniquely beautiful for a purpose. Let's truly be like Christ. Let's truly lay down our own will and do the will of the Father. He loved everyone, even the ones who were going to betray Him. He actually loved the ones who were close to Him. Do you know how many people outside of the 12 disciplines would have not betrayed Him? But, He still kept those who betrayed Him close. Jesus is the first and best example of one dying to self for the purpose of something greater, and that was to save the world.

Chapter 10

Warrior to Warrior Challenge

Before I conclude, I want to leave you with 22 Challenges that we must adhere to as warriors.

1. Make sure you set aside time to intercede daily.
2. Sharpen your armor daily, and use it throughout your daily walk with Christ.
3. Stay pure before the Lord.
4. Spend time with Holy Spirit daily.
5. Ask to start a prayer group on your job.
6. Ask your leaders if you could start a prayer group at church.
7. Surrender and address anything that could hold you back; this includes trauma. Do it, even if you need therapy, counseling or deliverance. Don't be

afraid of deliverance. Jesus delivered his children throughout the bible in many ways. We are his children.

8. Be wise at all times when having conversations so that you don't cross the threshold of gossip.

9. Make sure you have a group of intercessors you can be accountable with.

10. Create a list of hobbies and have fun.

11. Find time to fast weekly.

12. Love yourself and people. Please read, 1 Corinthians 13:1.

13. Repent and turn away from idols and iniquity so that you can honor the will of the Father.

14. Lead souls to Christ.

15. Worship and praise no matter the circumstance. A song of freedom from your belly can terrorize the enemy. In 1 Samuel 16:23, David ministered in the way of music for Saul.

16. Address any generational curse that

needs to be destroyed in your bloodline.

17. Mentorship.

18. Set time for consecration.

19. Your voice is a weapon. Travail! I remember being so heavy and I let out a travail and healing and revelation came instantly from God.

20. Continue to pray for your family, friends, church, enemies and nation.

21. Keep your head up, mighty warrior. Remain on post and cover the land in intercession as a pure vessel.

22. Stay Humble.

Prayers

Prayers over the Mind

Your Word says in Isaiah 26:3, "You will keep in perfect peace whose mind is stayed on you, because He trust in you." Lord, I thank You that my mind is focused on You. I destroy every thinking pattern that does not glorify You, including idolatrous thoughts. Make my mind over again. Your Word states in Romans 12:2, "And be not conformed to this world; but be ye transformed by the renewing of your mind, that ye may prove what is good, and acceptable and perfect, will of God." Lord, I decree and accept the peace that is rightfully mine in my mind. I cut off all the lies of the enemy. Today, I rip out all of the vocal cords of wickedness and follow Your voice and Your Word. I decree my mind is free and whole. I have a healthy mind. Lord, I invite You into my mind, actions and heart. Fill me up, Holy Spirit. I command my mind to be subject to the Holy Spirit. Lord, I receive this freedom, and will never turn back from it. Lord, I declare peace seven days a week, 365 days of the year. I will not live a day without peace. I will walk out of my door floating on the clouds of Your never-ending peace. I will sleep and eat in Your peace. My mind is free, in the name of Jesus. Amen.

Prayers Against the Spirit of Worry

Lord, I thank You that in Philippians 4:6, it states, "Do not be anxious about anything, but in every situation, by prayer and petition, with thanksgiving, present your request to God." Lord, You called me to a life of peace, righteousness and joy. I now sit and eat from Your table as a citizen of the Kingdom of God. Every thought that did not come from Your table, I overthrow, cast out and decree that it will return no more. Lord, I cast all my worries and cares upon You. You are already steps ahead in every situation. Lord, I have decided to trust You and put up my shield of faith. I know who holds my today, tomorrow and future. Matthew 6:25 states, "Therefore I tell you, do not worry about your life, what you will

162

eat or drink; or about your body, what you will wear. Is not life more than food, and the body more than clothes?" Lord, I completely leave everything that is causing me stress to You. I decree that You are lifting every weight of darkness off my chest right now. I receive Your love and confidence, knowing that You are in control. Father, I take off the burden of me trying to be God, and I give it to You. Lord, You are all-knowing and omnipresent. I believe that You are God in every area of my life. Let there be not one crack or crevice that You do not cover. Enter in, Mighty King, in Jesus' name. Amen.

Prayers against Heaviness

Lord, I thank You that Your Word says in Psalms 34:17-18, "When the righteous cry for help, the Lord hears and delivers them out of all their troubles. The Lord is near to the brokenhearted and saves the crushed in spirit." Lord, I know that You have met me on this day. Lord, my heart is heavy, and I decree that today, You have delivered me from heaviness. Isaiah 61:3 states, "To appoint unto them that mourn in Zion, to give unto them beauty for ashes, the oil of joy for mourning, the garment of praise for the spirit of heaviness, that they might be called trees of righteousness, the planting of the Lord, that He might be glorified." In advance, I celebrate knowing that I'm free and Your joy is my portion. Help me to rest, knowing that You are in control. Today, I decree that peace, joy and victory are mine. I lift my hands to You, knowing that You have poured the fresh oil of peace upon my head. Today is a new day. I arise and step out on the faith that Your love will carry me throughout the day. Lord, I drink from Your fountain of hope and joy. This drink will never run dry, just like You said to the Samaritan woman. Let this cup of joy I drink today run over until it blesses everyone around me, in Jesus name. Amen.

Prayers against Satanic Attacks

Lord, Your Word says in Matthew 16:19, "I will

give unto thee the keys of the kingdom of heaven: and whatsoever thou shalt bind on earth shall be bound in heaven: and whatsoever thou shalt loose on earth shall be loosed in heaven." I bind every spirit of darkness and wickedness that tries to bombard my mind. I take authority, in the name of Jesus, over any mind games, mind control spirits, and negative cycles, and I command them to break NOW! I decree that God's heavenly angels are surrounding me with protection. I repent for any unclean thought or unclean spirit that I have allowed to enter my mind. Your Word states in 2 Corinthians 10:5, "Casting down imaginations, and every high thing that exalteth itself against the knowledge of God, and bring into captivity, every thought to the obedience of Christ." Any imagination contrary to God's Word, I destroy it now, in the name of Jesus. Lord, let Your voice be amplified in my mind. I cut off any thought, idea or wickedness from the camp of the enemy that has been sent against me. Your Word says in Jeremiah 51:20,

"Thou art my battle axe and weapons of war: for with thee will I break in pieces the nations, and with thee will I destroy kingdoms." I destroy every dart from the kingdom of darkness and all wickedness that lurks around me and in me, by the power of God. Holy Spirit, fill me up and drench me in the love of the Father all over again. Drench my mind with Your love and Spirit, Father. Fill my mind, Lord, and drain out every thought that is contrary to Your Word. The enemy is defeated, and I'm undefeated. I receive my new dimension of freedom, hope and joy, in Jesus name. Amen.

Scriptures of Intercession

Romans 8:26:

- In the same way, the spirit helps us in our weakness. We do not know what we ought to pray for, but the spirit Himself intercedes for us through wordless groans.

Luke 23:34:

- Father, forgive them, for they don't know what they are doing.

James 5:16:

- Confess your faults one to another, and pray one to another, that ye may be healed. The effectual fervent prayer of a righteous man availeth much.

2 Chronicles 7:14:

- If my people, who are called by my name, will humble themselves and pray and seek my face and turn from their wicked ways, then I will hear from heaven, and I will forgive their sin and will heal their land.

Philippians 4:6:

- Do not be anxious about anything, but in every situation, by prayer and petition, with thanksgiving, present your request to God.

Ephesians 6:18:

- And pray in the Spirit on all occasions with all kinds of prayers and request. With this in mind, be alert and always keep on praying for the Lord's people.

Matthew 21:22:

- And whatever you ask in prayer, you will receive, if you have faith.

Matthew 5:24:

- Leave there thy gift before the altar, and go thy why. First be reconciled to thy brother, and then come and offer thy gift.

Acts 16:25:

- About midnight Paul and Silas were praying and singing hymns to God, and the other prisoners were listening to them. Suddenly there was such a violent earthquake that the foundations of the prison were shaken. At once all the prison doors flew open, and everyone's chains came loose.

1 Corinthians 13:1

- Though I speak with the tongues of men and of angels, but have not charity, I am become as sounding brass or a tinkling cymbal.

Bio

Sarah Flowers was born in Hamilton, Ohio to Rick and Mary Flowers. She has one brother named Ricky Flowers.

She received her Bachelors Degree at Miami University in Oxford, Ohio.

She received her license as a minister at Embassy City under the leadership of Apostle Bryan Meadows and Pastor Patrice Meadows.

She is a graduate of the Nehemiah School by Prophetess Joanne Goddard. She is also a graduate of Esther Prep University by Elder Tiffany Buckner.

She graduated from B.C.L.A., receiving her life coaching certification from Lakeisha Dixon.